Flirting with Women: How to Approach, Flirting, Talk, Attract, Dating and Seduce Women

Natalia Zimmerman

due to the information herein, either directly or indirectly. The author owns all copyrights not held by the publisher.

The information herein is provided for educational purposes exclusively and is universal. The presentation of the data is without contractual agreement or any kind of warranty assurance.

All trademarks inside this book are for clarifying purposes only and are possessed by the owners themselves, not allied with this document.

Disclaimer

All erudition supplied in this book are specified for educational and academic purpose only. The author is not in any way in charge of any outcomes that emerge from utilizing this book. Constructive efforts have been made to render information that is both precise and effective; however, the author is not to be held answerable for the accuracy or use/misuse of this information.

Foreword

I will like to thank you for taking the very first step of trusting me and deciding to purchase/read this life-transforming book. Thanks for investing your time and resources on this product.

I can assure you of precise outcomes if you will diligently follow the specific blueprint I lay bare in the information handbook you are currently checking out. It has transformed lives, and I firmly believe it will equally change your own life too.

All the information I provided in this Do It Yourself piece is easy to absorb and practice.

INTRODUCTION

At first, we would like to thank you for making this your own. As a man, you are to dream a dream of having a hot beautiful sexy girl as your girlfriend. You might be expensive, smart, intelligent, or handsome, but you can't just ask a lovely lady for a date without convincing her that you deserve her. If you do so, you will find the chance to be a successful deficient. This book can be the guideline for you to make her believe that either she is for you or you deserve her.

It does not mean that I am asking you to believe that it is a book of magic words. I am not claiming that after buying this book, thousands of lovely ladies will leap after you, and you will be dating them one after the other. The truth is that this book will tell you what you need to do and what you must not do to flirt the girl you want.

Another thing is that you should know that to have a date or a courting, you need to flirt with your dream woman. Cunning or look, you would not have purchased this book if you considered your financial capability.

I hope this book is going to give you every theory and practical to tease the beautiful girl you desire. This book is mainly on flirting with a lady. It also highlights how a man must boost himself to make sure that lovely women can observe him. We have also tried our best to allow the readers to know the kind of women that ought to be selected. As you have to choose the lady who suits you, and that can supply you with every little thing you desire from a lovely girl.

So, the book is somewhat qualified to act as the standard for a man to take him closer to his desire girl.

Teasing is necessary to get the girl.

If you can't tease or flirt, she'll see you as "just friends." There will zero sexual stress and zero attractions-- not what you desire.

Flirting is the difference between friendly conversation and sexual conversation. The difference between her seeing you as close friend zone product and her going weak at her knees for you

The power of flirting is suitably summarized in a quote from the television series Mad Men: "You have to let them know the type of man you are, then they'll know what kind of girl to be."

In other words, are you a great, pleasant person or a sex-related man? Are you a close friend zone product or lover material?

Currently, if you're reading this book, you're an awkward flirt. Or possibly you don't have the know-how to flirt at all.

That's okay, because despite appearing like a problematic principle to understanding (I mean, you just flirt., flirting is very simple. As soon as you get the remarkably simple core methods down pat, flirting is not only comfortable but fun.

Before we dive in proper, I wish to give you my sincerest congratulations for taking the very first step in a collection of favorable actions that you will require to absorb order to take control of your dating life. The essential things which you will learn right here regarding ladies and dating are things that I assure you most men in the entire world will not know about their female counterparts. You are offered expertise and information about the greatest keys women have. This consists of details on how ladies think. It includes information on what attracts ladies. It likewise provides info on how you can show the lady around you that you are a great catch, and they must stand and take notice. The book includes details on how to come close to a woman and how to speak to her or chat with her as well as how to keep her connected as you start dating her. There are dating pointers here that many men would disregard.

I make sure that you realize the reason why people will not go out of their way to discover information regarding any subject if they currently think that they have enough info to get the results they desire. After that, what happens when your approaches stop creating the results that you so prefer?

What happens when you recognize that as you age, your methods are not helping you at the same time? Well, at this factor, you have either options. You can choose to continue in your routines and keep doing whatever you are doing even if you know it isn't working well for you and simply expect different results. Or second, you can look for new information that can help you transform your existing behaviors and make much better choices in the future. Yes, the first of these alternatives is reasonably poor, but the second reveals an excellent sign of your character. And picking up this book is just one of those attractive signs!

Bear in mind that many guys proceed with the first (and bad) alternative. The irony of this thought is that it is the same reason why virtually all men fail to discover the most basic and efficient approaches for dating, which you will find in this book.

Happy dating!

CHAPTER ONE

Journey to Flirting

WHY FLIRT?

What's the point of creating sexual tension?

Well, if you don't create sexual tension, you'll probably end up being her friend.

You see, women are like a mirror. If you treat her and speak to her like a friend, you'll become her friend. If you treat her and talk to her like a sexy woman, somebody you wish to have sex with, you'll become her lover.

However, in any case, you will not end up wasting your time as her "friend.") And so, if you wish to bed women, not buddy women, developing sexual tension is a must.

And the best way to develop sexual tension is to flirt. And to flirt? Well, here are two of the best methods, starting with:

What is flirting?

An excellent place to get a response to this question would be the dictionary.

flirt

verb

1. act as though sexually brought into someone, but playfully as opposed to severe objectives

Why Flirt?

To address this inquiry, let's take a look at an instance of a discussion.

where there is no flirtation;

Guy: Where are you from?

Girl: Melbourne!

Guy: Australia? Wow. Did you manage to make it through all the deadly animals?

Girl: Yeah. Laughs.

Guy: Nah, seriously but, I've heard it's one of the world's most livable cities or something. Why would you relocate?

Girl: Yeah, it's a pretty fantastic place to live. I moved because ...".

Blah, blah, blah. And the conversation continues. Notice the problem?

In case you didn't, here's the answer: The conversation is entirely platonic. There is no sexual conversation whatsoever. For all we know, maybe two guys are talking.

To put it bluntly, the guy in the example conversation is going to be going home alone.

And so there you have it, the solution to why flirting is a necessary part of seduction. It gets her picturing the two of you with each other romantically and makes it clear in her mind that you're a sexual guy, not a "just close friends" kind of guy.

Okay, so if flirting is vital to getting ladies to see you as a guy to make love with, and not a "good friend," after that, why are most men nasty at flirting?

Why most Men Suck at Flirting

The men that stay clear of the blunder of not flirting at all (and thus ending up as "just friends"), usually make one of the following mistakes.

For you, this means that as you develop your flirting skills, you'll have another benefit when it comes to seducing the ladies.

Anyhow, here are one of the most typical mistakes people make when flirting

- THEY ARE TOO OBVIOUS.

Many men are simply way also noticeable when it comes to flirting. Why is this a problem?

It sucks the mystery out of the interaction. And along with that, the magic goes excitement. Intrigue is fun, but being obvious kills it.

Below's an example of clumsy, noticeable flirting:

Lady: I enjoy sports bras.

Man: I wager you 'd look outstanding in a sporting activities bra.

Ugh. As well obvious.

So what should flirting resemble instead?

Well, as you'll find in the following chapter, great flirting is much extra refined. It's done with implication rather than specifying things outright. It leaves other enigma and intrigue--more for women to guess about.

- THEY'RE TOO DIRECT.

Being extremely direct likewise kills the excitement of intrigue.

As an example, this is why it is usually foolish to compliment women based on their physical appearances. (E.g. "You have stunning eyes," or, "Wow, aren't you a stunner?" or, "Are you a model?") Apart from making it appear as though you've never been with an eye-catching lady before (an unattractive trait per se), you kill any mystery you have regarding your purposes.

On top of that, being too direct sexually,(e.g., "I'm going to fuck you so hard later") eliminates a woman's ability to absolve herself of feelings of sluttiness by reasoning that sex "simply happened." Females have been mingled to feel humiliation and fear about being perceived (by either herself, her friends, and even society at large) as "slutty" or sexually promiscuous. So when you're too straight with a woman you've just met and made it clear you're going to bang her, most females bring up some excuse or just disappear. You can consider this as their "anti-slut defense.".

What you need to do instead is give her the means to justify sex as something that "just happened"-- probable deniability. "I've got this amazing pool table at my place; we'll go play around." While you and she both understand what's likely to happen (hint: it begins with "f" and ends with "k"), this example gives her the means to reason it away. She can tell herself that she's merely going to your place to have some fun and see what happens rather than she's going to your site to have sex with you, which would leave her feeling slutty and dirty.

Anyway, so what's the lesson? Do not be so direct!

- **They use friendly chat rather than sex-related flirting.**

You people probably banter a lot if you have a group of male friends. Nevertheless, unless you're gay (which you're probably not if you're reading this book), the small talk isn't going to have any sexual undertones.

Regrettably, for many men, they use this same kind of non-sexual exchange when attempting to flirt.

For example, the difference between sexual and friendly (nonverbal) flirting, think about the difference between giving a girl a "high five" compare to holding hands. One is non-sexual, the other unmistakably sex-related.

Many people take a much less risky path rather than making a robust and high-risk action. This leaves the interactions they have with girls with no sexual undertone.

THE JOURNEY BEGIN.

Flirting with a woman can be a long trip. Sexual never matters excessive if you end up being effective at last. Some guys do not know where the journey should get going. Every man loves to have a chat with the lady he likes. The conversation might just be composed of official greetings like "Hi" and "Hello." Still, the chat can bring a lot of good feelings for him. At the same time, he has to keep in his mind that his journey of flirting with her starts with these official greetings. If your conversations go on and on consisting of just a vocative greeting, she might just put your name in her listing of close friends. She might think this person is just curious about making plain friendships. So you got to attempt to thrill her at your first glimpse. It is precious for you to make a date. You can directly send out the message having your intention if you start flirting with a female after being familiarized with her. You have to tell her directly or indirectly that you are not speaking with her only for making friendship. You need something more. You are asking her for a date. As a result, she will consider you differently than she thinks of other men. You can use all your tricks on her. As she has already had various views on you, now, your techniques of teasing will be confirmed more with the ability to encourage one day. Your journey will take off with a fantastic hope.

Firstly, in your journey, you may not get a cozy welcome from the lady of your dream. You have to be impressive and tranquil. You can not allow her to know how much you are trying to flirt with her. Flirting is a process in which at the end of the day, the lady ends up being desperate for a day. Do not ruin your difficult job by devoting many wrong actions.

Understanding Women.

The truth is that guys are virtually not aware of what a woman wants. Without knowing her like or desire, it is impossible to flirt with her. More or less females know very much about a man's wants.

There is no doubt that to flirt with a lady, you have to know what she desires, needs, and wishes. You can not have a date with a lovely woman unless she is impressed.

What women desire in a man

-They want Respect: Women always want respect from men. It is a common idea that is offered in guys that connection is such a thing require to be accomplished, and women can not get that. If the same reasoning is found in you, you can be classified as one of them who believes women as a requirement just for bed-life.

Mindset will indeed never show that you have got respect for them. Ladies can quickly recognize who respects them for real and who does not. Just start to admire them from the heart. Sooner you will discover most of the women are overlooking your other mistakes only for this top quality. They will begin showing interest in you. Even they might want you for their entire life as a partner. So, courting them will be more much easier for you.

-They Want A True Lover: You try the heart and spirit to show yourself as a real enthusiast to the beautiful woman you want to flirt with. Most of the situations, females do not agree to go for a date unless they find their companions love them.

-Make her believe that you can fix all her distresses: In this modern world, women are no more weak sex. Still, they love to believe that their man is qualified to fix any problem they could be passing through. To make her feel this way, you have to concentrate anytime she talks about any of her issues.

-Women like loving and serious guys: Most of the females seek their chances to have a connection with famous writers, actors, singers, and athletes. They like these renowned males because they understand these stars are enthusiastic and sincere. It means that they want their man not only in bed but also in leisure activities and professions.

Having known that you have got lots of interest. She might think that it is time to look at your enthusiasm in the real place, which lies where every woman wants their guy to be passionate most.

-Women want Mr. Dependable: Women are significantly independent nowadays. When it is time to choose a man, they usually neglect it. Every woman wants to depend on her guy and your desired woman, so does it. You try to be a reputable man for her. If you are trustworthy and reliable enough, it always easy to be positive about having a date with you. Because of this, you will have the ability to date her quickly. Firstly, you need to send her the message that you are reliable through your jobs. If your desired lady asks you to do anything for her, it can be sending out emails to someone, getting some books, opening a financial institution account-no issue just how much they look weird to you, try to do the work correctly. She will lose her belief in you if you make a mess of it. She may think she should not have asked you as you are not reliable. Therefore, she could lose some of the tastes she had for you.

-Ladies desire a Man with aPurpose: Women never choose aimless people, as every lady wants her guy eligible to be introduced. They enjoy gossiping. They love to tell others about the job, position, or requirement of their partner. For this, they consider a man having a high passion. So, to flirt with, you can tell her that you are relatively enthusiastic. Do not assume that she is going to think about your words unless she sees you striving to emerge your goal. Do not be late. Allow her to see you pushing hard to acquire an excellent task. Give more than100 percent of you to build a conformist career.

-Lady desires a mindful Guy: Women wish to be cared for. A woman wants his man to be cognizant of her. She desires her male to be caring about her job, research study, needs, and wellness. If her man is reckless about her, she plans to block the road of their relationship. When the game is over, she does not want to be a toy for her man that is thrown away. So you need to be very careful with the woman you intend to flirt with. If she tells you about her illness, you need to go to see her right away. You may stay far away from her, but you need to keep in touch with her in that situation. Speak with her over the phone. Inform her that you are quite worried about her, and you are going to fulfill her immediately. Let her feel that you are incredibly concerned and moved. Also, inform her that you have gone mad to see her. It will create a belief in her that you care for her. It will make her cheer and protected. She will desire this kind of love and treatment for a long time.

Women Need and Desire

Ladies like to desire. They are positive in a playful way. They always want their desire for their life, and they think their men will always get it materialized. It is time for you to discover the hope of the lady you intend to flirt with her.

-Female Enjoys Fairy Stories

We all know that females are warm of opera-soaps, T.V. programs, fairy stories, and charming novels. They want their life to be compared to a fairy story or an enchanting story. You need to allow your desired woman knows that you have come to bring her the best.

-Women Desire for a Hero

Women see a whole lot of Television shows. The lady you desire needs a hero like those programs in her real life. Your girl wants to be enjoyed like a hero enjoys the heroine in flicks or Television shows, and she desires you to be with her in every situation.

-Lady desires to be the best in his man's Eye

Ladies want to be attractive. She wishes her guy not to find another lady more beautiful than she is. If you're going to flirt with a girl, you must not commend the look or shape of another lady in her present.

-Ladies need financial protection

Or else, she might be worried about what her future is going to be if she remains with you. Females always look for economic security. When she understands that you have gotten the ability to satisfy her needs, she might not hesitate to go for a date with you.

-Females want you to be special

Possibly you are not a person that has something in you. Now you have to try to be unique. Ladies always want somebody special. Generally, when a man gets a chance to flirt with a lady, he asks for advice from his nearest and dearest people. The information is practically like "Be yourself "; Think about this guidance. They are of no use. If you do not cohangeyourself, there will be no difference between you and other men. This will not help you. You have to be different; otherwise, the girl you want will not find any type of particular factor for her to approve you as her date and deny others. So, you have to be unique.

A lady might have lots of friends, specifically male friends. Once she figures out that you are attempting something with the same strategies that are familiar to her to excite her, she may be disappointed. To flirt with her, you need to have a specialty in you. You need to be a person that she has never known. Bring changes in her life. To be unique, you need to be one-of-a-kind in every possible means. Expect, the lady you are looking for has invited most of her friends and you at her birthday party. All the invited friends will attend her birthday party with many birthday presents. You have to take it seriously. Invest enough time and get a gift that is going to be unique and gorgeous. Do not go for a ring or pendant. Those are pricey, however productive or not unusual for your purpose. You can go for a little puppy.

It will be proof of your unique and distinct choice. It might make her think about a different method about you. Hence, you can be a unique one for her.

There are some common subjects and tricks that guys use to impress a girl, and of course, they are well known to ladies by now. As you know, ladies have gotten tastes for flicks and enchanting stories; you may be caught. Females like innovative men.

How To Quickly and Easily Master The Art of flirting

Okay, admittedly, this may look a little bit corny in the beginning, right? I get it. You do not think that you need a personal development tutorial on pseudo-pop-psychology. You believe that the way you see the world is just great. You may be thinking, hurry up and simply tell me how to start flirting and get speaking to women; why in the world has he began talking about the change of mind; why would I need to consider things or check out things differently? Because it's damn important, that's why!

Below are the things; if you watch the world in a certain way, your entire mindset starts to change. Your attitude or the way you assume, whether good or bad, can transform everything in your life.

Favorable psychology scientists are finding that assuming beneficial thoughts and sensations pleasant emotions can help in anxiety management, boost overall health and wellness and well being, and even enhance social and professional skills. Thinking favorably and doing tasks that make you experience positive feelings, not just gives you an instant increase, but the impacts can last much longer after that. Researchers call this the 'widen and build' concept. When you assume favorably or experience excellent feelings, your mind is open to a lot of new opportunities. In an article on the science of hopefulness, James Clear discusses that this, "in turn enables you to construct new abilities and resources that can supply worth in other areas of your life." For you, this suggests that by believing favorably and eliminating negative thoughts and uncertainty, you can get much better at flirting and start attracting more ladies. Potentially even being with something real and significant, if that is what you are after.

Yes, depending on the way you are feeling, you are either sending out an adverse or favorable message to women and everyone. This is why, before we begin anything in this book, you should understand the impact of ideas and how to get assuming positively.

In the simplest terms, if you believe that you can not do it or you are adverse or always anxious, after that, you are setting yourself up for failure. If you are positive and make a selection to delight in life and live it to the fullest, after that, good things will happen. You will give yourself extra chances for success.

Do you wish to find out how to speak with ladies? Do you intend to be confident enough to flirt and even get more dates? Start by developing the appropriate mindset. What have you reached loose? Altering your mindset will drastically change your love life permanently!

The best spot to start is by having a look at how you've been with ladies in previous connections. When you have a good suggestion of what you want, you can see an emphasis on the favorable facets of a person you wish to date and consequently enhance the probabilities of coming close to her and successfully flirting with the right woman.

CHAPTER TWO

Self-development

"Self-Development" offers you more opportunities to flirt with a girl. The fact is you can't change your appearance entirely according to your dream. You may be a guy of a typical occurrence. You can flirt with beautiful women by developing your personality and speaking manner if you wish. These two qualities of a guy have the ability to impress a woman. When you are on a mission to flirt with a girl, these two qualities in you can help you a lot to win your desired girl.

Character advancement.

Your personality is such a thing that can surpass all of your qualities. It creates beauty. You can not establish your nature, just keeping in mind some processes or theories of character development. You need to use whatever you know at the right place and time.

Be Punctual.

Women like punctual people. Do not keep them waiting. If you need some more time to fulfill her than you told her, ask forgiveness from her and just inform her that you are going to be late that day. She might consider you favorably. Do not do it often. If you do so, she may consider it as your wrong usual and you an insincere individual. Punctuality is a fundamental part of your personality.

All set for an outing.

Sitting in a place all the time can make your girl bore. You better take her out. If you are only eager to sit with her in a room, she might consider you a person who does not like to engage with too many things.

Don't ask her many personal questions.

It is a common thing. It destroys your total character. Your desired girl will never like you if you need to know her stuff from her. Nevertheless, you might have the interest, but you better hide them as much as possible. If you can create enough chem, she will open herself as much as you in no time.

Speaking manner.

To flirt with a girl, you must be perfect in your speaking way. Your speaking way can help your desired girl to separate you from other men. Some essential aspects of stabilizing an excellent manner through your speaking are given below:

-Manly Voice.

To flirt with a good looking lady, you got to use your voice completely. Some people have a gifted voice. Their view is deep and positive. This type of view is pleasant to flirt with stunning ladies. Women typically love this kind of male voice. When you discover yourself lacking this manly positive voice, the issue emerges. Still, there is no need to be disappointed. You can make it up. Stand in front of a mirror and start speaking to yourself. Try to get a manly, confident, and deep voice out of your vocal organ. Nowadays, long conversations over phones are very typical between young men and young ladies. Because of this, flirting can be very easy for those who have turned their voice into a developed one.

Less quantity of slung.

When you are flirting with a woman, you can not do it. You can discover other signs of her speech.

You can use double-meaning jokes.

That will be funny to her when you are in front of her and in an early stage of flirting with her; at the same time, you need to be careful about not using slung especially. It might bring a wrong impression on her if you slung exceptionally often in the presence of her. She may think of you negatively. She might avoid you and consider you a bad man and a hot temper. Avoid this habit. Try to be funny. It can be advantageous if you are now a funny man who has a fantastic sense of humor and breaks jokes so often. Women like this sort of man. You can go one action ahead by keeping a smile on her face. You can not create the interest of your desired girl in you unless you make her smile by doing something hilarious.

Don't be too ridiculous.

Sometimes you might act silly to make her laugh. This is never great for you. You need to know that a beautiful woman might choose a ridiculous person only to laugh at all times. Your girl is to date a guy. So, you can not function as a silly person. For this, you need to avoid silly jokes to start with, as ridiculous jokes can typically end up being boring and horrible and make you look immature.

Start talking after she has finished speaking.

You always talk after your girl is completed. Never interrupt her while she is talking. Girls never allow this. They take it as an embarrassment. You might need to wait for long as women love to talk more. If you start talking while she is saying something, she will lose her strength to talk. So, let her talk till she is not done with talking. It will tell her that you have a genuinely excellent way of speaking.

Tease her Often.

Teasing her through your words might be helpful for you to flirt with her. Women like to be teased often by their closest persons but not to be teased in the manner that may disgust her. Remember it; your teasing needs to entertain her. You can tease her, highlighting some kind of sexual meaning out of her words. It can tell her what you are up to.

Confidence.

Self-confidence means your faith in your ability. You must have this quality if you desire to date or court a woman. A guy having confidence is ahead of others in flirting with a woman. When a guy is asked about things he desires in the woman with who he is going to make a date, the possible answer is that she must be beautiful, hot, and attractive. If a woman asks the same question, the reasonable response will be a good-looking and positive man. So, there is no alternative to confidence when you want to flirt with a stunning lady. You need to express through your attitude that you are a guy having an excellent quantity of confidence in yourself whenever you are with the girl you desire.

Increase your self-confidence Level.

To raise your level of confidence, at first, you need to believe yourself better than others in every sphere of life. You will be an exceptional change. Immediately your appearance or your approach towards women will be changed. It will begin to show confidence in you. Some men can not have the courage to flirt with a hot girl. They merely believe that they do not deserve them because they do not have some qualities women want. Get rid of this type of belief as early as possible. Even if you do not have something, you can manage them in time. There is no point in getting disappointed. Be positive and begin to think that you are capable of courting any beautiful girl.

Look Confident.

To look favorable in the eyes of women, you need to bring some changes in your standing, strolling, and making eye contact. As your reputation and strolling typically offer the idea to others about your self-confidence level, you need to do those stated act effectively and very smartly to show self-confidence in you.

As first, you need to make sure that you are getting assistance from nowhere when you are standing. I mean, gradually stand up without leaning. Your weight should be brought by both legs equally. As a result, you will not slump. Slouching is not for them who are positive.

Stroll with the best rate. While strolling serves as a tough guy. Your standing will mean that you do not care about anybody or anything. To get an example of strolling with self-confidence, you can see any popular motion picture where you will find the man standing with confidence.

Over self-confidence.

Overconfidence can work against you. Having a high level of confidence does not mean that you can disregard anybody you like. Always try to stay down. Some men inform their ladies that they are very positive about flirting with the women to show a level of their confidence. Generally, it never works. Women think that they, men simply want to have fun with them. As you know, women always want love; they will never tolerate this type of man. By making this kind of mistake, a guy himself stops his journey to make a date.

The Mindset

To develop a positive mindset, take a minute to consider how you presently feel when you approach a woman. What sort of words entered your mind? For me, it used to be words like a clumsy, bumbling, strange, worried wreck, dirty shoes, wrinkly t-shirt, no aftershave, lousy hair, halitosis, awful, etc. What do you discover? Possibly a bit of an underlying theme of negativeness? I'm ready to bet you if you are honest with yourself, you presently have your variation of negative self-talk and that you believe you could not potentially approach her or that you will get turned down? This kind of unfavorable self-talk is like a self-fulfilling prophecy and, in turn, will likely dictate your result. If you doubted yourself or lacked self-confidence, then you were shooting yourself down before you even started. Your mindset is everything; therefore, it's time to begin feeling excellent about yourself and your flirting approach. Change the unfavorable words with the positive and watch what happens.

Try replacing one unfavorable thought with a positive and view the magic happen.

Attempt stating I can approach that woman. Try looking at the mirror and tell yourself something that you like about your look. Dig deep and develop your most positive characteristics and attributes. This is introspective and might be tough or silly, but I promise you that if you try it, you will open something truly fantastic within you. Doing this will also help you approach and draw in the best woman who is searching for the same favorable qualities you possess. Just try to change one negative belief with a positive one and see how it transform your whole outlook and the reversed sex's outlook towards you!

Society portrays women as the only ones who deal with being positive. Stereotypically, it's presumed that men are simply born positive and, therefore, favorable, but this isn't real. The reality is that men struggle with a favorable mindset and self-love just as much as women. It may not be as spoken about, but it's a problem, on the other hand.

If you're trying to change your dating game or at least be much better with approaching women, then it all starts right here and today. All of it begins with you feeling good about you. Good things will start to happen when you make the shift. Women will start to take notice and will be captivated to see what your positivity is all about. A positive, confident guy is very appealing. You can not only get the kind of relationship you want but likewise produce the life that you always want

Once and for all, just choose to change your mindset!

Take-aways:

- Creating a favorable state of mind is extremely important as it will increase your chances of flirting successfully.

- Positive thinking can help in tension management; improve overall wellness and health, and produce new life skills. Your new skill is flirting!

- Positive mindsets are attractive to women (and men if you want more friends).

You can create a positive frame of mind by:

o Using the advantages and disadvantages of past relationships to focus on the favorable qualities of a woman you now desire.

o Replacing negative thoughts and words with positive ones.

o Focusing on forecasting your highest.

o Removing unfavorable self-talk to allow you to be effective.

Improving Appearance

If you are too short, you can not be tall in a month.

If your eyes are too small, you can not bring them in an ideal size.

As we know, these things are gifted. You can not change them to improve your appearance. Enhancing your presentation is all about looking your best. Women never miss any sort of small information in men's looks. So, you are to keep your look perfect if you wish to impress your desired girl.

To flirt with a girl, you do not need to be the best-looking person in the world. Just attempt to get the best of you. In this case, a cute hairstyle, smart looking clothing, getting in good shape, and keeping you clean and fresh can be more than useful.

-Clip Your Nails and Get rid of Unwanted Hair

Women like tidy people. They never allow a dirty one for flirting with them. So, keep yourself neat. Clip your nails regularly. Suppose you are with the girl, the girl you wish to flirt with. All of a sudden, you offer her a glass of beverage how will she feel seeing your nails too long and ultimately dirt; it will not be a great scene for her. You, yourself, will also miss some things you need to impress her. You also need to get rid of unwanted hair of your nose and ears, as they often damage the freshness of your look. To flirt with a girl, try your best to look fresh and fit. In this matter, a shower before going to meet your desired girl will help you a lot. A shower helps everyone to look fresh; Your freshness will attract her.

-Get in A decent shape

I am not saying that you need to have a body like a design or a wrestler to flirt with a girl. You simply require a decent body figure. If you are too fat or thin, women will simply not pay much attention to you. They do not like men who run out of shape. If you currently have a good body, you can be granted as fortunate. Somebody who does not have it needs to work a bit on it. Try to cut down a few of your weight if you are fat.

On the other hand, you require to get a reasonable amount of weight if you are too thin. You can likewise take the help of an excellent trainer to have a good and balanced physique. Accomplish it, and after that, you will discover more women are getting interested in you.

Have a Cool Hair Cut

Women prefer men who have an elegant and up-to-date haircut. Get a hairstyle that fits your look and hair best. A stylish haircut will make you more attractive to the girl you are flirting with. Even an elegant hairstyle will refrain from doing if you do not look after your hair. So, get the right haircut and make your hair look great so that you can draw in the girl you wish to flirt with.

TheSame Clothing in Consecutive Days

Women discover all your look. If you use the same clothes in more than two successive days, your desired girl will notice it ultimately. Women do not like this practice. You might never see a woman who uses the same gown for successive days. They likewise expect the same thing from you. So, do not use the same clothing for consecutive days. Before going to bed, you can choose your next day's dress. Requirement Outfits is vital for you to flirt with the ladies. Great clothes always have a terrific effect on others. Ensure whenever you are in front of your desired girl, your clothing is clean.

Use pleasant smelling mouthwash and fragrance

Always utilize an excellent smelling mouthwash. It will provide you with the self-confidence of getting closer to the girl you want to flirt with. Suppose you have picked a date with her, if you have the confidence of getting your lip closer to her, you will not get the opportunity to kiss her. On the other hand, if she receives a great smell coming from your mouth, she will be interested in coming closer to you. Thus, you will have a perfect date. Use excellent mouthwash and keep yourself set.

A great perfume or a deodorant can offer you the same type of benefits.

Do not forget to use your perfume and antiperspirant before going out.

The things I have told you so far to improve your look are not merely all. Look out for more that can be contributed to make you a better-looking person.

Fear of Rejection

Let me tell you a story about a male. A man fell for a hot and gorgeous girl. He wished to court her at any cost. At the same time, he was scared of getting declined as a result; he stayed quiet. As usual, his silence might not bring him any good news. After a couple of days, he came to know that one of his close friends was attempting to flirt with her. After some days, his friend ended up being effective in courting that beautiful girl. At this news, he was injured terribly, but it was too late for him.

This is a familiar story. Men who have a fear of getting declined, they get the same results the man of the story. You can not escape the outcome of the man in the story unless you get rid of the worry of rejection.

Conquer this fear today

You can easily enjoy the appeal of many beautiful women standing by your window. You can not date any of them by standing there. So, you need to leave your space and be committed to one of the stunning women. As you know by now, after getting engaged, you can start flirting with her. Men who worry about rejection feel that women will let them down. This fear will never let you be with a gorgeous woman. So, overcome it.

A man who is experiencing this fear must understand that he, himself, is developing this fear. He needs to inform himself that getting declined by a beautiful girl is not the end of the world. It happens to everybody; you just need to mature. He needs to take opportunities to flirt with girls. It will be a waste of a chance if he gets turned down. As a man, he is expected to flirt with a girl he desires. Likewise, as a hot woman who you want wishes to be somebody's date. So, the probability of becoming effective is more than being a failure. There is no point in only looking at your desired girl from a distance and getting upset when someone else goes for a date with her. Forgetting every fear, you had better start striking on her today before anybody makes you his competitor.

Just Go With It

All of us know that shit happens. So, being a person, not preferred by luck, you can be turned down from a woman. You must accept it and not be distressed. Maybe the woman who has declined you is simply not "your type." You must carry on with your life and start hoping for the better. Do not stop dreaming of a date with a lovely lady. Once implies missing out one chance, I have already said that getting rejected. Attempt to find out from your previous mistakes and prepare yourself to flirt with another girl once again. Be optimistic while flirting with ladies. Do not be hopeless.

There is always a better one waiting for you. Consider rejection as a chance to get a more stunning girl than that person who declined you. Simply go with it; you are now a mature man.

Be Choosy

Yes, you are a handsome young guy, and you are terribly in need of a woman to make a date. Whatever the situation is, you have to be picky. Unless you end up being selective about discovering your appointment, you can not get a girl of your type. You need to guarantee that the girl you prefer is worthy of all the hard work, money, and time you have invested for her. Because men always run after the appeal of the women, her outlook might interest you most. At the same, you have to learn some other qualities in her that can give you joy. If you do not discover the following attributes in your girl, you better look for another girl who has the following qualities.

-Always sincere to you

Sincerity is an essential quality in a relationship that is required for you to believe her. After becoming your sweetheart, you can ask her many questions to test her whether she is truthful with you or not. Ask her about her person and family life before she becomes your sweetheart. You understand women love to talk. Sooner or later, she may say the fact. So, if she had lied to you, you could have caught her.

-Love you more than your job and money

Women always desire a glamorous life and a better future. For this reason, they prefer rich men. In some cases, lots of gorgeous women pretend to live a rich man or a man having a good job. If you are rich or doing a good job, you need to ensure that your desired girl is not a woman of that type. You can not choose a woman who enjoys your wealth more than you.

Another crucial thing is you must select a woman who listens to your words. Do not just do what she asks you to do. Discover how much validity she holds for you.

-Trusts you a lot

Ensure that the girl you are flirting with trusts you a lot. She is yet to fall in love with you if she does not trust you. Make another thing sure that if she shares every trick of her life to you and something that she has never informed anyone previously. If she shares, she is your girl because women only share their secrets with their confidant and reputable persons.

Be interested in passing more time with you

You should take her out to have some annoyance downtime with her. You need to discover how many times she has asked you for an outing. The more she asks, the more she is interested in you. Choose someone who wishes to have more time with you.

CHAPTER THREE

Learn How to Create that Fun and Flirty Vibes

The primary step in flirting with women is ensuring you begin on the right foot. Your first impression will develop the speed for the rest of your interaction.

You need to comply with some basic rules from the beginning to build the love they keep the mystery and want.

RULE # 1: Don't outrightly show your interest. Most women do not want you to walk up and make a declaration that they are interested in them. That is boring. -- they are already aware.

And how do they become aware?

Because you are in a way showing interest by talking to them, that is enough sign. If you attempt to tell them you are interested directly, it kills the romance.

Men are different from women in aspects of social conduct. Women will talk to any man or girl about anything—even strangers. Guys will just speak with people if there is a reason. If you are talking to a girl as a man, you are surely interested.

RULE # 2: Get going with the flirty vibe. You would like to use humor as a way to begin the flirty vibe. You wish to seem lively, but you also want her to continue doubting whether you love her.

When you generate an atmosphere where she comes back at your comments with some jabs of her own, you can create sexual stress. This is basic psychology. Arousal is stimulation. This is why you might have had a few of the best sex after a significant fight because any friction can create stimulation.

RULE # 3: Confidence is one of the sexiest things you can have. Absolutely nothing is sexier to a woman than you being confident. While it might help your opportunities to have a great deal of money or huge muscles, you can still land an attractive and desirable woman without those things so long as you are confident.

The quantity of confidence you have is built from your interaction and the amount of attraction you can create with a girl.

One of the ways of being confident is making eye contact. Another part is having excellent posture. When you are talking to her, be sure to use her name. Lastly, it is essential to put on a passionate tone. If you end up sounding bored, she will believe you are.

Now you require to make these things a regular part of your character. They expect to stream as easily as a smile. They need to be authentic. That authentic self-confidence comes at putting a high value on who you are as a person.

You can't get phony this. She will see through it rapidly. You have to develop this self-confidence by approaching each new interaction with the state of mind that it does not matter whether she is drawn into you. The less you care, the much better. Tell yourself that you require nothing from her, and it does not matter if she likes you. This is where real self-confidence begins to establish. It looks like a detrimental idea, but it isn't. This will give you the inner confidence needed to play the indirect flirting game women love-- without always further guessing yourself and looking at how well you are doing.

Finally, make sure to take it to a physical level as soon as possible.

Getting From Verbal Flirting to Physical Flirting Fast!

Physical contact is a great way to construct a connection. Physical contact is a great unspoken kind of interaction that clearly states you are interested but keeps the mystery that women love.

Physical contact is good, but it should not be for more than a couple of seconds. A light touch can inform the woman that you are comfortable being close to her. It informs her that you find her attractive. That you are comfy making love, If she touches you in return, it tells her that you are interested in her, and it is okay.

Unlike the other people who have approached her, you are going to leave her wondering:

He hasn't directly said anything, but he appears to be heading out of his way to show he is interested.

He hasn't attempted to impress me, but he keeps touching me, does he like me or not?

This is a significant difference between women and men. Men hate guessing whether or not a woman is interested. If things are uncertain, it pisses men off.

Women are the opposite.

They love the blended signals because it keeps them on their toes. It keeps her thinking.

It gives her a challenge. And most significantly, it is from someone who may not need her attraction.

I make sure you are starting to see that the laws of a destination vary considerably between men and women. Women don't appreciate a man who is too offered. This comes off as a clingy puppy. They also don't desire the all-business direct approach because that eliminates any prospective secret or romance.

You have to be mindful of the indirect approach. It can, in some cases, come off as meek. You want to develop a destination, but you must avoid coming off as meek. You require the slightest "bad young boy" image to build a magnetic tourist attraction.

The fascinating destination is something more powerful than you can imagine. It is the type of target where women can not control.

If you desire to improve your dating life, you require to develop this destination.

Conversation

They say women love to talk. To flirt with a woman, you have to speak to her. Some excellent discussion can impress her easily. Women always try to find men who talk well so that they can have suitable feedback. If you ever get an opportunity to discuss with the girl, you will need to get the best out of that conversation so that she gets interested in you. Below are strategies that will help you to make your discussion fascinating, more protracted, and satisfying to your desired girl.

-Make it longer

Try to talk for a long time whenever you speak to a woman. So, do not offer her the opportunity to finish the discussion with the aid of just two or one "YES" and "NO." You need to ask her questions that will make her talk much to respond. The more she talks with you, the more she gets open up to you. This is what you desire. You ought to give her time when she is making a lengthy conversation, even though her details are not relevant. Do not disappoint her. She may think that you are giving your valuable time just to hear her problems. It may bring luck to you.

Attend to her words

A male always wants to state something that may impress her desired girl. As he takes part in the discussion, he starts to think about what his next sentence is going to be while his girl goes on speaking. It might work against him. As his brain tries to find out what his following sentence is going to be, he can not attend to her words. When the girl finished, he can not connect, or in some cases, he needs to say something irrelevant. This event produces an odd matter for the guy and the lady. So, his desired girl does not get any interest in this type of conversation. He needs to change his conversation technique. He needs to pay a quantity of concentration to the words of his girl so that he can include something pertinent when she finished. As a result, the conversation can move on, ideally.

Be her Assistant

You become the guide for her. Whenever you take your preferred girl to a new place, you manage her. The scenario is different in conversation. When a discussion goes on, the girl rests on the driving seat, not the male. There are two factors behind it. One is, women love to talk, and the other is that women talk much better and organized. Let her speak and just help her so that she can enjoy her talking. After she finished, you can tell her," ultimately said," or "you are satisfied." Such comments will inspire her to talk more to you. She might consider you to be the right person she has been trying to find. If it happens, you are more than a fortunate person.

Usage little Hints

If you wish to have a conversation with a beautiful woman, you can use "little point," she will give you. : you are in a coffee store. All of a sudden, you discover a charming girl in the coffee store. You might have a chat like this:

You: I am much regular in this store. Unfortunately, I have not seen you before.

She: I am new in this town for a research study purpose.

If you use little tip here like "research study purpose," you can make the conversation proceed by asking her about College or

University. Therefore your conversation is going to be longer and worthwhile.

Don't bring topic she does not Like

This is a common mistake that nearly every man makes. You ought to not pick subjects for discussion that you like instead, you need to choose items that she likes while discussing with your desired girl. If you bring the subject you want and simply go on talking about it, she will get tired if she does not like the topic. Next time she will reconsider before starting a conversation with you. You better try to understand her favorite topics to discuss. You are a massive fan of football, and your desired girl does not like it that much. She does not have that much understanding of football. If you start talking about what happened last night in the English Premier League, she will merely get no interest in your talking and lose hope in making conversation with you on that subject. It will significantly harm your work. These are the essential things you do not desire.

The less she talks, the less you have opportunities to flirt with her. So, discuss some topics that she likes, and she has a reasonable understanding of that topic. Only then will she show any interest in talking to you. Thus fruitful discussion goes on. You can speak about Television shows, magazines and so on as women primarily favor these subjects. If you do not find any interest in these things, you have to pretend. You need to keep in mind that you are up to something. This is just a little sacrifice for your mission, and it can bring you good luck with a chance of having a date with her.

The power of "Me Too."

Women prefer men who have almost the same kind of disliking and tastes they possess. They delight in the scene whenever a male supports their concepts and ideas. If you want to be close to her or if you want to flirt with her, you need to develop the routines of uttering the two words, "me too." These two words are strong enough to get a woman's loveliness. These two words from you after saying may need her to think that finally, she has got a man who holds the same kind of likings and disliking as her.

Better not use other lines

While viewing movies or checking out a story, you may find some gorgeous dialogues or lines. You may think you can use any of these to impress the girl who you wish to flirt with. Honestly stating it is exceptionally risky. As you understand women like romance novels and movies, she may determine where you have managed it. Kindly tell her with attractive lines or dialogues, which is the author of those lines or conversations if you do this. And inform her that you also think like this about her. Never try to copy other's paths and make them your own.

Be honest (Women like honesty)- They will never compromise sincerity for anything.

 It will create a wrong impression on her. You better depend on your own words. Women love self-dependent and imaginative people.

Make the Move

Just flirting with a beautiful girl can not get satisfaction for any man. He wishes to date her. So, earlier or later, you need to make a move. After being sure about her preferences for you, you can ask her for a trip. When you offer her a date, you ought to look positive. It is much better not to use sentences include words "might," "would," and so on. To draw out my point, I can give you a couple of examples:

You: Can we choose a trip? Please address me.

Or,

You: It is time for us to opt for a trip? What do you think?

You will discover the second one more manly and positive if you compare these two examples. Women want their men to be masculine and confident. So, the second one has more possibility of getting an affirmative reply.

A time will come when the girl who you are flirting with may want you to ask for a date. If you are reluctant or make it late, she will believe that you do not desire it, or you are not brave enough. She will attempt to discover someone else. Do not make it too late.

CHAPTER FOUR

Flirting Do's and Don't

Understanding how to flirt with women can bring substantial changes to your life. Through flirting, many women will believe that you are a fun guy to be with and will want to hang out with you more. If used in the right way, it can even lead to more serious relationships. Men have been flirting with women and vice versa for thousands of years. It is an entirely natural leisure activity.

A lot of flirting includes making the woman feel excellent; the intention must not have to do with sex. By making another person feel pleased, you will also feel more positive about yourself. There are many places that you can flirt; there are social gatherings, workplaces, even when you are traveling.

To start with, you need to know how to use your body movement. By standing close to a woman when talking, and making expressive gestures and casual contact, you will develop a better bond. When talking, it is not wrong to touch a woman on the arm occasionally. As a rule, women are typically more physical than men; therefore do not mind contact unless it is in an overtly sexual nature.

If you are in a congested space, then you can use eye contact to flirt with a woman who might be some distance away. Then interest will develop, and you can approach her if you keep smiling in her instructions and make eye contact over a few hours.

When you fulfill a woman for the first time, avoid cheesy chat lines. Even if she is a stunningly gorgeous woman, you ought to be as natural as possible; complimenting the way she is dressed will make any woman happy!

Flirting with women is a skill that can quickly be developed by any guy. It may take some practice, but ultimately, you will begin to see the results.

Things not to Do

You ought to be technical to approach a woman. There are specific things you need to desist from doing. In this chapter, I will be speaking about the things you need to refrain from doing.

-Do not be too readily available

Try to present yourself as an extremely busy guy in the Eye of your desired girl. Even if you are not busy, you should pretend to be active. By presenting yourself as a busy person, you show that you are leading a life that has more interest. She will know that you are giving her your valuable time only to make her happy. She may be convinced to be with you. Never make yourself that readily available to her.

If she does not make a relationship with you, never tell her that you will be ended up. It will show a weaker personality of you to her. She might not like it. You may be psychological, but do not reveal your complete emotion to her. Women themselves do not like girl type emotional men. You had better avoid this.

After flirting with her for an extended period, you might get used to her interest in you. You should observe her a little bit more if you get the feeling she likes you. If again, you find out that she likes you, but not telling you about her feelings, do not make more hold-up; you need to ask her for a date. Women want to go on a date by men. She might like you, but she waits for you to offer her.

-Never make any commitment

To impress her or to flirt with your desired girl, you can tell her that you are always ready to do anything for her. You better not involve in any commitment with her. She may believe that she has bought you if you get involved in any responsibility with her. Do not be included in dedication.

It is better to not talk for a long time over the phone

You might want to have a discussion when your desired girl over the cell phone when she is not with you. It is prevalent for every guy.

You might have a chat for one or two minutes. You must not talk on the phone for an extended period. It will make her feel that you are someone who has nothing to do but discussing on the phone for hours.

-Never get jealous

You might find your desired girl having time with another person. You may not like the scene as fast as possible you need to conceal your emotion.

Your expression must not reveal that you are jealous.

You must pretend that you are quite liberal about this matter.

You have no business in their relationship. Your jealousy will let her know your possessiveness.

-Women do not like possessive men.

Whenever you are with the girl who you are flirting with, do not pay attention to other gorgeous girls. As you are trying to make, her comprehend that she is the only girl that can make you go crazy. If you are looking at other girls more than her, she will consider you a scam, even a pervert. This is not an excellent thing for your mission. Once again, women are possessive about their relationship, although they do not like possessive men. So, do not spoil all your hard work making this kind of mistake.

Warning!

-Do not attempt to flirt with women at the funeral service.

- Do not try to flirt with a girl who already has another half or boyfriend.

Most Significant Mistakes Men Make.

Imagine if we were to place a group of random men into a room together and ask each person to say the typical mistakes guys make with ladies, that they are personally guilty of. What would happen?

A man by nature is well delighted to confess their faults when it comes to dating, particularly honestly in the presence of strangers. The first guy may have a difficult time acquiring numbers while the second guy has a problem with keeping women interested. The next person can have a fear of coming close to ladies.

While another man scares ladies away by being an asshole and does not know he's doing it.

Every single one of them would definitely have something that is either difficult or might be boosted.

Do you even recognize the most significant errors males make with ladies?

How you address those issues does not matter, because no matter what you think now you'll be thinking entirely in a different way by the time you finish reading this list of the top 5 greatest mistakes men make with females and some guidelines to assist curve these harmful routines.

1) Staying in your relationship zone.

That's right, highest on the listing of mistakes men make with women is falling to get beyond their comfort zone and try the new things that are needed to broaden their game along with development. Abandoning your comfort zone is among the hardest achievement when it comes to meeting and dating girls. This is what differentiates the young boys from the men, and the men from the real men. That's due to the reality that it requires extreme games.

Whether it's approaching, intensifying, shutting, or another thing, most of these things are out of the usual for many people, and overcoming this fear of the unknown is the first step to conquer. When you read many success stories and also reach the part where the man begins to improve rapidly, that's typically when he finally breaks out of his comfort zone. That's when a new world opens.

The most useful advice I can give you is to push yourself, but that's all the tips you'll ever require. Press yourself to be incredible, press on your own to make mistakes, media to your straight-out limits. After that, you'll know that what you thought were your restrictions isn't even close to the fact, and you can take it more and if you just keep at it. I'm not going to exist. This process will end up being extremely hard at times, and you'll begin to yearn for the pleasant comfort of mediocrity, but you need to be consistent. The outcomes will come, but just to those that I've gotten it and given it everything they had.

You need to ask yourself:

" Am I going to risk of the regular to accomplish the exceptional?".

Establish your places of interest high and never choose less than you deserve.

Always bear in mind that; If you strive to boost yourself and also your flirt game, after that, you will get results that show the initiative that you are.

That's precisely how the game is played.

2) Being a cock!

Oh yeah, this is a large one. Why would being an asshole be second on our list of mistakes people make with girls? For novices, due to the truth that it usually arises from men attempting to boost their game, not make it tougher to flourish. Many people that are just starting learning more about seduction end up being a considerable penis to a great deal of the ladies they try to flirt.

Why?

This is simple to identify, however not so easy to break the regimen as soon as you have already acquired it. Mostly, when people first locate this web site is among the most attractive ways they find are the ones related to teasing and badgering women. This is because these can get you fast outcomes contrasted to the majority of the different other things, and that doesn't like getting what they want as soon as possible? There's no worry about that, yet it can turn into one when you spend last time improving those methods without making use of anything which is meant to balance it out.

For instance, if you are high at creating and teasing ladies

Don't recognize how to construct comfort and connection; think about what occurs? It makes you look like an asshole. Whether it works against timing or being severe, new men always end up doing it too much. If you push a lady away excessive without knowing how to reel her back in, that's precisely what you're doing at some point:

-Pushing her away forever.

There's no definitive option for this. You merely need to discover your balance by practicing a variety of methods rather than just focusing

on one. That stability varies from man to man, depending on your uniqueness. Some guys can escape more teasing, while others have an easier time creating comfort. The more you practice and establish your flirting game, the more you'll discover more about on your own and also how you need to personalize your game to fit your design and strengths.

Always bear in mind that teasing isn't recommended to be your support approach.

The original goal of it is to construct the first itinerant aim, and you ought to try hard until you achieve your objective,especially when you notice that she is attracted to you it's time to tone it down (not stop entirely, simply unwind a bit)

and also start developing some rapport to work everything out.

You don't want to torture a girl, simply tease her adequate to differentiate yourself from the losers who do not have the spheres to wait on her a bit.

That's as far as it ought to go.

-Teasing excessive is among the biggest mistakes people make with females too often. Make sure to discover appropriate stability in your overall flirting game, so you avoid this significant risk!

3) Concentrating on getting laid

Vagina !!!!!

How helpful is that to you?

Among the awful blunders, men make with women is putting every focus on the wrong objectives and allowing it to handle their concepts and behavior. Generally, that goal is acquiring pussy. If your primary target, just getting laid, making that your crucial emphasis within your mind will genuinely screw with your capacity to run your computer game effectively.

There's no need thinking about it while you're with a female,

as that can limit the chances targeted at getting

the woman right into bed when you need to be using your full ability. When you go out wishing to meet females, some instances of great objectives to have are:

-Enjoying, satisfying people, enhancing your computer game as well as boosting your social worth.

Some cases of contrary goals when you go out to meet women to have are:

Getting laid this night, the number of times you get, flaunting, and resembling you're the guy.

Because this does not mean those are the wrong objectives to have, fairly the contrary. They're wrong to focus too much. Merely by going out to having fun and meet new ladies, you'll be getting great deals of numbers, looking like the man to getting laid. It's about your state of mind.

4) Putting cuffs on a woman.

Guys that are just finding the game tend to get recorded captivated with the first woman that they successfully use their new skills on. This is among the typical errors guys make with women that can be exceptionally hard to be clear of if you're new to these things. They after that, they concentrate on that specific one girl that they overlook to keep exercising and also advancing their game. They assume they're done.

There's nothing wrong with falling in love, and it is possible that the very first woman you achieve success at shutting can be "the one."

You'll forget every little thing if you allow one woman to manage your sincerity you know about the real game and start making a shitload of blunders, such as:

You'll try to keep tabs on what she's doing.

Acquire jealous worrying different other guys being around her.

Fret about her leaving you or wearying.

Do everything she wants to like her little bitch.

The paradox behind this is that you'll be making all of these blunders to stay away from something unfavorable occurrence. Yet, your characters will be what makes things you are afraid od end up taking place for real.

When you get a lady, the game does not end. It's just started.

5) Promising, not giving.

I've observed that a lot of people will state things like:

" Yeah, I'm conceited."

" Money isn't an issue for me."

Or "I'm mean too sure for that."

Rather than showing their beneficial qualities through their doings, some ignorant men will try to express them to thrill women. This is one of the greatest blunders men make with women, however one that can be quickly avoided. That's why it's just number 5 if you aren't boasting.

Deliberately, you need not to describe your enticing vocally.

Do not reveal your qualities to a woman. It's a bad idea. Instead, show her through your actions.

Throughout the PUA area, we tend to spray words like "player" and "confident" as well as "alpha," but you ought not to directly notify a girl you're any one of those things. It will not impress or attract her.

If that had not, doing so will make it look like you're bragging even been your function. Believe me; if you are a cocky, specific guy who has a lot of money, you have no reason to say it.

Just by communicating with a woman for a while, she will detect and discover each of those things on her own, which is the natural action it should take and will make a better perception to her. What you assume is much more impressive to a woman, telling her you have a Range Rover when you first met or appearing in your Range Rover along with shocking her when you check out to pick her up for the first day? The only reliable way to verbally provide your excellent traits is by telling stories instead of being so specific.

Doing it in this manner will typically stop it from getting the bragging label because the essential things that you say are simply "a part of the story." However, that isn't the best means to do it; if you want a girl to know something surprising about you, revealing it to her will be better than trying to notify her about it.

Well, there you have it, the leading five mistakes men prevent them.

The Rule of Flirting

Don'ts:

Do not appeal to get the desire or regard of a woman. This means no buying her drinks at a bar or offer to drive totally out of your ways for her. There is no reasoning dealing with a girl that you have fact just known for a couple of weeks like a princess. You ought to go ahead and make an actual observation to guarantee she is putting forth a minimum of 50% of the effort in keeping the long-term relationship.

-Don'tplace her on a pedestal.

Recognize that you as well have worth and needs to work towards.

-Don't be scared to disagree or tease her playfully. It's necessary to activate the position in her. It shows that you have self-confidence; it helps prevent you from putting her on a stand. She's a human being with concerns & problems much like everyone else.

-Don't tell a girl too much about only how you feel ahead of time in the relationship. -Mainstream media will always ask you to share your feelings and say to the woman how you feel. This is a substantial mistake, as she will certainly see you as a weak doormat.

Do not speak to her on the phone, message, or Facebook for hours at a time.

Always have something much better to do than hang around talking with a woman, such as using a false time restraint to leave conversation where possible. The principle is to leave them on a high note, advocating more. SMS message and call need only to be scheduled for specified days and meetings as well as talking with her in reality.

-Do not over-analyze everything. An example consists of "OMG, she touched my leg. She wants me," Girls can tell when you're into them, and you need to have the ability to say if they enjoy you. Suppose you can't know if she enjoys you; after that, more than likely, she's not.

-Don't ask her what movie too she wishes to see or where she hopes to have dinner.

Take control and decide for both of you. Women desire you to take control and lead the interactions. Don't be 'wishy-washy' and indecisive!

Don't go extremely out of your way to do things for her. Act to her as you 'd act to a friend about favors. Treat her as an individual.

Do not hesitate to rip their clothing off, bend them over a chair £ the crap out of them often. On a subconscious degree, all females like to be dominated by a reliable person-- just as long as she is saved with him. Women might be the fairer sex, but they are not made from glass as long as it is done in a method which she enjoys and is pleasing for her.

Dos:

-Do act with confidence in any circumstance, especially if you're not especially outstanding looking. Otherwise, you are sunk from the start.

You can move on many ladders that you might not come across in the past. That being said, you need to get her focus at first. All that's required is confidence and being comfortable in your very own skin.

Pre-planned lines nearly never work. A simple "Hi," will work as long as she likes you.

-Do be busy with other things in life, whether that is family friends, working, doing pastimes, or dating different other ladies. Women want to see that you are the kind of person that is in need, whether it be from various other women, companies, or friends. Likewise, if you need to make shit, that's better than being always readily available.

Supply & demand idea, similar to basic service economics. She won't like chasing you if you are often chasing her. Give her the present of missing you.

-Do pleasantly reduce to make boyfriends things with her till after you are barely hooking-up and dating. This recommends at least full-make-out sessions. Not holding hands, cuddling, or pecks on the lips. She will attempt to regulate the framework early on and have you jumping through her hoops. Managing the frame is essential.

-Do learn to be watchful for the little things that reveal enthusiasm. She isn't going to jump on you and tongue tussle you show her interest.

Instead, she'll stay longer than essential when talking with you, she'll poke fun at unexpected jokes, she'll play with her hair, lean or angle herself in the direction of you, and playfully strike you or touch your arm.

-Do tell her only 1/3 of the shit that you plan to say to her. Ask her flexible queries & after that, shut your mouth and let her yell on. When she asks you questions, be funny/witty, and keep your actions shorter. The only solution maybe 1/2 of the question she asked. This is how you stay, "magical.".

Do always remember that there are different other women out there, just as appealing, captivating, and fresh as the one you're having now if you aren't satisfied by taking care of her (either she isn't giving or being demanding), after that by all means just leave and find another woman who will provide you with less issues.

-Do show your feeling with actions, not words—this related to what we examined earlier. Do not share your opinions vocally when any type of woman friends or member of the family asks you to "tell her simply how you feel." If you never plan to see her when more? After that, go right ahead.

What females state they want (a guy that reveals his experiences) and likewise what.

She responds to are two different things. Expressing your feelings for her will transform her off as fast as a light switch.

Do magnify physically when you seem like it. Not when you believe she looks like it. Like we said, "she's not made from a glass," and you need to show her you are physically generated to her. Be lively, be specific, and go for it!

CHAPTER FIVE

Crucial Flirting Tips for Men

The majority of men out there deal with the one big issue that they are not able to flirt with women. Because they do not understand how to flirt with women, lots of songs are frustrated. And it is a significant reason why they're single. Well, here is a set of vital flirting tips for men. Use these tips to bring in women and fill up your solitude.

Do you know flirting is everything about giving - not to get. What are the things you need to 'GIVE' women to 'GET' something from them? Well, is this question too hard? Think once again. You have to give what they have to get what you need. Women like compliment and care; they want to be treated like women. This is the essential flirting advice for men, simply give women these two things, and you will have lots of women to flirt.

Many women want somebody to lead them in their lives.

They want someone to lead them to make decisions. And it's just a woman nature. If you're asking how to flirt with women, then you should establish an ability to lead women on their ways.

Touch a woman as you're her friend - When you have developed a little intimacy with a woman, then you can increase that intimacy by touching her. You're closer to feel her feelings if you physically touch her. So, you should contact her in natural manners frequently. When you lead her, the best timing to affect a woman materially and create emotional attraction is. When she is about to make a big decision, hold her hands.

Hold her hand when you lead her through a crowd. Now you will get her mentally hooked on you. Congratulations.

You require to know the whole flirting technique to use these tips to a useful life. And once you know how to flirt with women, you'll get on your method to draw in a lot of women to seduce.

Flirting Tips You Can Use Today to Attract Women

Have you ever seemed like the topic of flirting seems to be a total mystery to you? Have you felt like you have no idea and unaware of what makes a woman brought in to you? Don't be discouraged as you are not alone if you think this way. Because it is not something that we have been encouraged to do, the majority of men are not that good when it comes to the art of flirting.

So how can you start discovering how to flirt with women to get them drawn into you? Here are tips you can use to help you get going today:

1. Tease her

Teasing is among the most effective techniques when it comes to flirting with women, but it is also probably among the most overlooked methods. A lot of men try to show their interest to the woman they like by showering her with compliments, compliments, and more compliments. Think about how uninteresting this is to a beautiful woman who has been listening to comparable remarks for their whole life? It will show that you are a man of high social value and yet still show to them that you are interested in them if you use a teasing approach instead.

2. Touching her playfully

Without a doubt, the most direct and best way to communicate interest in anybody is through touch. The problem with this is that most men are not comfy with this because they have been taught when they were young that sexuality is the only kind of intimacy that is appropriate for a man. Just take a look at how hardly ever men hug each other as compared to women, and you will get what I mean.

3. Facial expressions

A lot of men have been told to smile more as a way of flirting with women. Smiling too much can, in some cases, backfire and make you come off as clingy and a "great man" what you need to instead mix your smiles with subtle expressions such as laughs, playful winks, narrowing of the eyes, or any other emotions that express some kind of inner thought. This leaves the woman trying to think about what you truly mean, and it can genuinely help to stimulate some interest!

4. Subtle sexuality

Don't let the cultural stereotypes from the media and your environment fool you. There is no doubt that women love sex as much as men do, but they are probably only not comfortable with saying it out due to stereotypes. But if you can discuss it subtly and leave her thinking, you can be sure that she won't stop thinking about you.

There are lots of men who never learn how to flirt with women very well. They look and sound ridiculous, striking up a woman with a corny line or, at best, "Can I buy you a drink?" It's no surprise that a lot of men feel awkward and clueless when it comes to drawing women's attention.

Do you need to know how to flirt with women? Are you truly tired of being rejected because you're approaching them the same way every other man they fulfill is approaching them? Making and smiling eye contact may make her a little less anxious that you're not an ax murderer, but it isn't going to make you stick out in the crowd. It's like many sheep standing around the bar, bleating. What you truly need is these little-known tips to bring in women by flirting. Not only will they be less ridiculous-sounding, but women will also notice them and you a breath of fresh air.

-No More Mr. Nice Guy

It's challenging to flirt with women and have success until you have at least an idea as to how attraction works for them. Women are drawn to men who make them feel safe and a little intrigued at the same time. They don't want men who bend backward to please them at every turn. You're going to end up with a considerable chiropractic doctor's expense and no date if you're the latter.

Think about this: Would you feel secure in the company of someone who did whatever you desired them to do, precisely the way you wanted it done, without ever questioning you or thinking for themselves. One would hope not! Of course, it's accessible to boss around that kind of person, but you'll be tired to tears in no time. Women can identify a spineless jellyfish very quickly. Women desire manly men, not pushovers. If you are always 100 percent acceptable and obedient to her every impulse, she'll soon realize you don't have any self-esteem. He can be badgered, not only by her but by everybody.

This goes against most of what you've been taught about women, but stop being Mr. Nice Guy 24/7. This is probably one of the essential tips for dating you will ever learn. Find out to jeopardize, but not all the time. Often, things need to go the way YOU desire them to go.

Other Tips

Be Unpredictable

If you want a woman to feel safe and secure, how is it possible to create a balance between security and a bit of conspiracy? You don't want to bore her to tears by being a doormat, but you don't want to be viewed as an overbearing jerk, either. The best way to achieve this is to include a little unpredictability occasionally, and a touch of mystery. Leave her guessing for a bit. It is essential to balance this out with duty and self-confidence.

The best way to achieve this is to keep your life, your character, and your worths simply as they are, even if they aren't accurately made to her orders. You may lose some due to this, but you may also be amazed at how much more some women will want you when they realize your desire can't control you.

You're not the only guy contending for the attention of a lovely woman, which means she's now in the habit of having men leap when she snaps her fingers so that they can keep her attention. Women can get bored with this constant pandering, so if you genuinely want her attention, let her know in little ways that while you 'd be pleased to be part of her life, you also have a mind of your own, and you intend to use it. This will set you apart from the rest of the flock of sheep following her, bleating. A little bit of unpredictability can be an excellent thing.

What, you ask, is the final dating signal?

When She Tests You, teasing Her

Now you understand that women end up being tired with a man who does exactly what they want when they want, you're asking why a lot of women want their men to leap when they whistle. It's quite simple: She's evaluating to see if a man is brave enough to walk up to her, or if he's merely cowardly—the majority of men who fail this test end up in the "just friends" classification.

It's easy to determine these tests. Most times, they are completely unreasonable or ridiculous. The best way to "pass this kind of analysis is to tease her gently for being silly. Doing this automatically brings you to the head of the class.

Using these guidelines will make it possible for you to take pleasure in a substantial distinction in your dating life. Your male friends will be lining up to ask you what in the world you're doing differently because unexpectedly, you'll be the one who known how to flirt with women.

Tips of Flirting with Body Language

Flirting isn't bad, particularly if you understand how to do it right. When you flirt, and you'll be pleased to realize that people like it when someone is doing the flirts with them, it is quite hot. It is a way of regarding individuals; it has something to do with smiling, whispering, and touching. As soon as you do it best and in the right environments, it is a potent tool to attract the attention of your date. Do it in the wrong situation; you'll be declined.

Here are some ways to flirt using eye contact:

o Pupils can be dilated while attempting to preserve eye contact

o Eye contact together with arched eye eyebrow looks attractive

o Fast eye motion with a blinking

o Any type of winking

o Eye contact by which the gaze is held longer than the usual occasion.

Here is somebody language that means flirting:

o Thrusting the chest outwards while at the same time holding your gaze to your date.

o Mirroring or the copying of gestures that your partner would do

o Holding your stare while at the same time doing the rhythm of the music

o Having the legs crossed towards your date

o Display of flesh arm

You can do these things discussed above, but it is essential to understand the willingness of your appointment. When you flirt, then you better stop so you will not turn her off, in case he does not like it. You need to see the signs just to be sure.

How to Flirt With Women - Flirting Tips for Shy Guys

Among the most challenging things for a guy to the divine is when a woman is interested. Women are more careful than men and wait a while to indicate that there is potentially some interest. Read those words thoroughly - possibly some interest. Women usually don't leap into things. So how do you understand when to pursue?

Generally, men have been the aggressor, but I can assure you that is not always the very best technique. Sure, be aggressive, but do it gently, and be ready to back off if you want to have success. Lots of women will simply shut you out if you persist when they have not shown some interest, or have made it clear that they are not interested.

How to Flirt With Women-Flirting Tips for Shy Guys

-Cultivate a Confidant - One right approach is to expect negatives in conversation. If, during your getting-to-know-you discussion, there are many topics that you think differently, then perhaps you will be friends and not "intimate" friends. If you know of an approaching instance that she may like, do it and wait on a response. Now, there is an idea - remain on an answer. This can likewise be a way of learning some things she does not like.

A good thing to remember is that a long-term relationship is based on relationships, not just desire. There is absolutely nothing incorrect with lust-- without it, a number of us would not be here. You must keep in mind that your woman buddy, considerable other, enthusiast, whatever, will be a pal and confidant as well as all the other excellent things. You need to have the ability to slam each other, share tricks, share good things, and evil. Somebody once said that a good friend is somebody whose faults you understand and you love them anyhow. That is not to state that every single thing needs to be shared. Who among us does not have a skeleton or two? Beware what you share-- it will not always be a good idea. Besides, why would you want to reveal something hurtful? Simply be honest in all things, and then you don't have to fret.

-Don't Be a Sore Loser

As men, you should realize that women are not always interested even if they are interested. This harkens back to the principle of dealing with women with equanimity. The most desirable and beautiful woman may just not have an interest in you. It does not necessarily mean there is anything wrong with you-- she may like a different kind of male. I have heard a lot of men compete that a certain woman is "foolish" because she did not give him a tumble. Well, just think of that and examine who is being dumb. The thing to do is to be friendly with her, and keep your eye peeled for someone else who might be thinking about you. Never annoy the woman who rejected you.

At the end of the day, if a woman is keen on you, she will find a way to let you know. Things will happen if you are smart enough to see the sign and act on it. If you are not, it's your loss. So keep your eyes open and your brain in equipment. Be open to all possibilities and be ready to act upon them. Don't push yourself on anyone, especially women!

Tried And Tested Tips On How To Flirt With Women And Get Sexual

You have approached her. You've talked for sometimes, and it's clear that she's enjoying it. Even better, she's comfortable with you.

What are you going to do next?

Well, guess what: it's time for flirting and stepping things up as far as sexuality is concerned. After all, the reason why you approached her is to get to know her "within and out." This is something that the average chump disregards.

They don't escalate and get stuck. All they could get is that minor peck on the chick. And when he tries to advance (way too late now), the girl responds: "Let's just be a friend. I believe we're better off that way."

You sure don't want that, do you? If you are struggling, if you don't know how to flirt with women and make her feel comfortable in your sexuality, the following tips ought to get you started in the right orders.

- How To Flirt With Women Tip 1

Before anything else, you need to have this mindset: speaking about sex is typical; it's cool! People do it daily. Making love and talking about it is similar to speaking about the weather—nothing fancy, nothing complicated, and absolutely nothing to be worried about.

- How To Flirt With Women Tip 2

Drop sexual overtones. Tease her a lot! Twist what she says and accuse her of attempting to seduce you. This needs to be carried out appropriately and excellently. Keep it enjoyable and light-hearted, that's what flirting with a girl is all about.

- How To Flirt With Women Tip 3

Discuss the future. This is among the techniques I love the most! By talking about a future event where you and she would be making love, you are not just implanting that idea into her head. You are enhancing the idea that you, together with doing the 'deed' is just a matter of time.

- How To Flirt With Women Tip 4

Be detailed, be very descriptive! This one is a little bit advanced. Likewise, you need to make sure that your babe is comfortable with your sexuality. By being detailed, you are developing a comprehensive and very sensual vision of you and her getting on it.

How to Flirt With Women - Tips to Ensure You Will Never Be Lonely

Are you one of those people who just does not know how to flirt with women? Are your attempts at flirting consulted with tepid interest at the very maximum, but more frequently with straight-out rejection? You have to do something to cure the situation immediately else you will end up lonely and depressed. It is an outright misconception that you can do nothing to improve your social abilities, and particularly ones that will help you interact with the opposite sex. You don't even need to be vibrant or good looking to be successful with women as long as you know how to talk with them quite well.

Flirting with women is an art, and you can find out the fundamentals of it. You can do much better than that and become truly successful in your interactions with women as long as you have the right training on how to flirt with women.

When they try to flirt, lots of men are too rigid. There is very limited opportunity for this succeeding because many women find this kind of habit very off-putting. What you need to be able to represent is an image of self-esteem, but need not stumble on as big-headed or pushy. You must also be as natural as possible because there is plenty of fish out in the sea and you will find more than one woman who wishes to be with a man like you. You are not likely to appear worried or required if you just be your natural self, and this is something that the opposite sex will find lovely. The confidence you obtain from having this knowledge will make you more adventurous and attractive.

Flirting is more about having a fantastic discussion rather than attempting to pressurize a woman to go out with you. Since this will make you very interesting to the women you meet, you need to develop the skill of being an excellent listener. They will be extremely grateful to open up to you, and you will get lots of chances to ask them out. This does not mean that you need to sit there silently. When the time comes, practice all kinds of vital things to say so that you are ready. Make sure that you get all possible information on how to flirt with women so that you can talk with any attractive woman you see without worrying about rejection.

Three Closely Guarded Techniques on How to Flirt with Women Revealed!

If you want to be active with lovely women, understanding how to flirt with women is vital. Women love flirting with men who know what they're doing. So if your flirting skills include saying "Hello there," and nothing more, you need some assistance. If you take note of the three carefully secured methods, you're going to enjoy more success with women than you're presently having.

1. Become A Bad Boy

Forget about being a good man. Bad boys are where it's at. Women love bad boys, even though they may state they're looking for a good guy. Often women report something but do the overall reverse. If you're not sure about what a woman is saying, look carefully at her actions.

Women love enjoyment, secret, and romance in their lives and think that bad boys can perform. They likewise wish to feel safe when they're out on a date with a guy. Since bad boys have credibility for being their man, a woman will feel safe when she's out with a bad young boy.

The last person, a woman, wishes to date is a wimp. Sadly, sometimes women correspond nice guys with sissies. So if you want to understand how to flirt with women, try to be more of a bad boy.

2. Excite Her With Your Unpredictability

This tip advances from being a bad kid. Women love the unpredictability, along with enjoyment and romance. Make her wonder if you're going to request for her phone number when you first meet her - your method may work so well that she'll end up asking for your number instead!

Being unforeseeable does not mean standing her up at the last minute, however.

3. When You Flirt, have Fun

A lot of men deal with flirting as a chore - and after that wonder why they're not active with women! If you need to know how to flirt with women, then you need to take pleasure in the actual practice.

Have a good time speaking to her and ensure you enter her private area - not so close that she can smell your breath, but near enough, so you can connect and touch her jewelry or her bag. Enjoyable, flirty movements like these are essential to a successful flirting method.

If you include the previous tips into your flirting efforts, you're sure to get a better reaction than if you follow what you're already doing (which isn't working).

These three carefully protected methods have just shown you how to flirt with women. If your techniques aren't working, why not try these instead? All you are required to do is get out there and practice till they end up being a force of habit. Accept your inner bad boy, end up being unpredictable, and enjoy flirting with beautiful women. Pretty soon, you're going to be among those cool people who understand how to flirt with women!

CHAPTER SIX

Why Flirting and Other are Related Matters

Flirting and fun are carefully associated. Since flirting, when specified loosely, merely implies fun and intriguing way of telling somebody you like that you are interested in them, this is. When you get into a room filled with people, and you barely know anyone there, you may be bored, especially if you are not the flirting type. However, if you like, you can flirt the entire evening with people you barely know without it turning into something simple. If you get to talking to some of the people you were flirting within the room and you feel that you liked them, you can tease yourself to a first date and maybe a long and delighted relationship. Relationships I will always firmly insist are begun with flirts.

Flirting and body movement is also quite judiciously related. Many people will always start flirting with somebody they hardly know by giving one body movement. The body languages I am talking about are the eyes, eye eyebrows, the mouth, the legs, and the hair. An individual will see a person in a gathering, and the first body movement they are going to send is going to be the eyes. They will look at them and smile that way; the person will get the info that the person wants to be familiar with them a little. They can retaliate with a sign of their own if they like them. Another flirting gesture that is going to be used by the woman is that of playing with their hair. If a woman likes you, she is going to play with her hair. Flipping it every long shot, she gets to show it off. A woman's hair is her priced belongings, and by having fun with it, she understands for sure that you will discover and see that she is a fun person to be with.

Flirting and jealousy are also slightly related, particularly in partners. This is because given that flirting is so much enjoyable, people who are in relationships do not wish to be left. This does not mean that individuals they are in relationships with will understand that they are flirting harmlessly, and they do not mean any damage to come to their method. Whenever a partner notices the other flirting with someone of the opposite sex, they get so envious. They can not say why they are flirting while they are in a relationship. When you want to start flirting, ensure that your partner is agreeable to the idea of you flirting with somebody else. Converse that it does not mean anything which could improve the relationship between the two of you.

Flirting and self-confidence are also closely related. A confident individual goes a long way in attaining something. Flirting has been known to increase a person's confidence by a very significant portion. Those people who are shy are motivated to flirt because it will boost their confidence. Flirting has likewise been related to enhancing people's relationship and sex life.

How to Use Conversation to Establish a Deep Connection with Her

Here are some of the most persuasive psychological topics you'll wish to go to when producing a deep emotional connection with a woman you're having a conversation with.

CONNECTING TOPIC # 1: EXPERIENCES

Our experiences are deeply tied to feeling. Whether youth, travel experiences, quitting a job and pursuing a risky new professional course, or anything of the type, our experiences are tied to emotions.

Here are some examples of methods you can get her to open about some of her experiences:

" What was it that made you desire to move to this city?" "What huge experiences have you been on?"

" What's the most interesting place you've traveled to?"

Talking to her about experiences she's had frequently cause amazing stories and stacks of emotion. More importantly than that, diving into the feelings behind her experiences opens up unique ways for you and her to relate to each other.

Here are some relevant examples of ways you might dive more into the feeling behind such experiences:

" How did it feel to do [X]."

" What was it like when you did [X]."

When it comes to associating with her experiences, you need not be scared, not having done the specific same things as her. Once you dive much more in-depth and get her opening up about how she felt about particular experiences, you can relate with her with various skills that triggered you to feel the same feelings.

So, for example, she may say that she stopped her corporate job and became a tour guide on some tropical island. When you dive deeper, she'll most likely reveal that she felt anxious and anxious about whether it 'd be all for the best-- weather she 'd regret it all as a "big mistake" and wish she stuck to her corporate job.

Now, you might not have done anything comparable, but you've probably been in a situation where you've felt similar emotions. For example, you may have moved from another country, began a business, or something of the kind. You can relate to her on an emotional level.

That said, don't endlessly drone on about your experiences. Briefly relate it to an experience you've had in your life (if relevant), and after that, flip the spotlight back on her. This allows her to understand that you "get her" and that you're listening and taking interest-- and that, heck, you guys are sort of comparable in some methods. But at the same time, you avoid being practically silent the whole conversation and having her start doubting that you're even focusing on what she needs to say or that you "get her." going on from the past (experiences), the next emotional subject is based on the present ...

CONNECTING TOPIC # 2: PASSIONS.

What are your passions? What do you love doing?

Scuba diving? Building organizations? Tinkering in the garage? Taking a trip?

Dealing with innovative engineering tasks at work?

Whatever it is, I desire you to think about it for a moment. Seriously. If merely for a 2nd, stop reading and just thinking of whatever it is you love to do.

Now that you've believed about that, how do you feel? How do you think when you consider whatever it is you love to do?

Probably great?

Well, women are no different when they are discussing anything.

It is what they love to do-- their passions-- they associate those positive feelings with being around you.

Here are some examples of ways you can get her discussing her passions:

" What do you love doing?".

" What sort of activities get you truly thrilled?" "What are you incredibly passionate about?".

And, once again, you can naturally dive into the emotions behind her passions.

Here are some examples of how you might do that: "What is it about [X] you love?".

" How do you feel when doing [X]" "Why are you enthusiastic about [X]."

You might find that you can quickly get her talking about her enthusiasm relate (and thus get in touch with her)--particularly if you both love to do the same kinds of things. (Note: Don't pretend you like to do something if you don't, she'll quickly have the ability to tell you're devising, and it'll just come off as extremely clingy, unattractive, and off-putting.), moving from the past (experiences) to the present (enthusiasm), the next psychological topic connects to the future.

CONNECTING TOPIC # 3: ASPIRATIONS.

Her objectives. Her hopes. Her dreams. What does she want to do in life?

People think of their dreams, but seldom get the possibility to speak about.

Because many people don't believe in asking, them, getting her to open up about her aspirations increases a whole bunch of pleasant, confident emotions-- all of which she'll unconsciously relate to you.

Here are some ways you can dive into this topic:

" What are your biggest goals?".

" What kind of things have you always wished to do?" "What are you aiming to achieve this year?".

Here are some ways you can dive into the feelings and emotions, related to her hopes and dreams:

" How would you feel if you did that?".

" What would your life look like if you accomplished that/'.

Carrying on, we've discussed emotional conversation subjects based on past, present, and future. Now, let's take a look at another sensitive topic that's more internal ...

CONNECTING TOPIC # 4: MOTIVATIONS.

Why does she do what she does? What makes her desire what she wants?

What encourages her? The vast bulk of people never dig this deep ...

Here are some questions you can ask to dive into this topic:

" What made you go for that?" (I.e., her college major or profession.)

"Why do that?" (I.e., what made her do/choose something she did, an excellent question to ask if she's telling you a story, etc.) You can dive even more in-depth with issues such as:

" How do you feel now that you're doing [X]" "What made you want to achieve [X]."

IT'S ALL A BALANCING ACT.

Previously on in this book, you discovered the best techniques for becoming a tempting flirt. In this chapter, you've found how to get in touch with women on a psychological level genuinely maybe the hardest part is neither the flirting nor the linking, but rather balancing the two.

If all you do is flirt, she may enjoy it at that time, but she'll probably end up flaking on you and even just forgetting you completely. There's no connection.

On the other hand, if all you do is have deep conversations and connect emotionally, she'll see you as a "just friends," and you'll end up being her pal, not enthusiast.

Balance the two so you produce both sexual tension and emotional connection.

INTENSIFY, ESCALATE, ESCALATE.

On the interwebs lives a funny little group called "NoFap." As the name implies, these are men that avoid porn, masturbation, and (self- administered) orgasm. (They refer to this as "PMO" for brief.) These so-called "astronauts" often say that, for some reason, they find themselves being successful more with women.

Imagine you have not orgasmed in days, weeks, or even months. You're going to be a horny mofo, right?

And, when you're connecting with attractive women, you're going to be more aggressive. You're not going to sit around have a respectful discussion only. You're going to attempt (whether knowingly or unknowingly) to take that woman to bed as soon as possible. Their horny nature makes them seduce women faster and more aggressively.

Now, why on earth and I telling you this bizarre story?

Here's why: I don't want you to make the mistake of stopping working from escalating the interaction.

You can flirt with a woman endlessly and speak to her forever about a gazillion emotionally-charged subjects. If you don't aggressively escalate the interaction and get intimate, it will all be for naught.

Lesson: Don't just talk and flirt. Get close or, at the minimum, get her number and set up a time to "get a drink/coffee." Be bold, be quick, be gone. Don't be around forever without escalating the interaction.

Take a Good Flirt Quiz - Do You Enjoy the TheFlavor Of Love?
The flavor of love is to love and be loved back. It is considered as the charm of love. If you love somebody who does not reciprocate your feelings, it is very heartbreaking. How do you tell whether somebody is into you? Does valuing your hairdo enough as a sign that somebody has an interest in you? The level of a relationship between two people will be told by how they flirt. If they flirt a lot, the general public concludes that there true love in their relationship. It is not always that a flirt turns out to be a romantic offer, but if there is an already existing dating relationship, the level of flirting needs to show the development. This can be done by taking an excellent flirt quiz.

For extra relationship effectiveness, you should have the ability to flirt more. Flirtation draws out the taste of love in many relationships and marriages. Some married people do not acknowledge the power of flirting. Top on the list of a good flirt quiz needs to question your behavior in your spouse's presence. Do you flirt with her more? Or do you use words or just body language flirting towards your spouse? If you flirt all the time to make her feel unique, you may be doing that, but always ensure that the flirt is from genuine observation. An overstated flirtation makes you look insincere and a non-serious enthusiast. If you do not flirt at all, you may be causing your partner to feel unappreciated—some couples do away with flirting as soon as they produce children. The kids should not work as an inhibitor in your being flirtatious.

All the partners need to know that if you do not flirt routinely with your loved one, somebody else somewhere will do that. Because it will be a unique treatment, she/he will react to it. If something romantic is made up, who is to be blamed? When someone else flirts with your girlfriend or partner in your presence, a good flirt quiz ought to question your response. It is a clear sign that you are not a liberated lover if you respond with a lot of hostility. I am not dismissing jealousy, but you must trust your partner to follow you. The incoming flirtation serves to validate your words, and because they will not be new to her ears, she will say something like "thank you" without a lot of excitement or "I am aware." Won't this make you proud? Of course, it will assure you that your partner delights in the real taste of love.

On the other hand, if the response to the question on the flirt quiz on the list is a magnificent smile to acknowledge the appreciation, you are a loving sweetheart or a husband. The taste of love is in knowing that you are appreciated when your spouse ultimately believes in you. It is the best feeling in the whole world. You should have the ability to flirt with another woman in her presence. If somebody is smart and you tell her so, this will make her believe in you too.

CHAPTER SEVEN

Your Approach

This the only way to change things

Okay, possibly that tail end was a little extreme on you. In some cases, reality needs to bite a bit, though, to enact change. However, I don't wish you to start unfavorable self-talk or feel rotten about the state of current affairs. The purpose of this book is not to make you feel dreadful or like you did something wrong. It's for you to find out and learn from previous mistakes. It's just currently you might not even know that you were doing things wrong. Maybe its that you don't even recognize where your game is entirely breaking down? Or perhaps you have been your own harshest critic, and it's not as bad as you think. However, you chose out this book for a reason, so it's time to break things down much more and get real with yourself.

Uncertain of how to do that? Feel unpredictable when it comes to finding out what you even need to be real about? However, if you tried honestly making a note of the qualities you desire from a future partner, then you have made a good start! Now we will try examining, in a little bit more detail, the next step in mastering the art of flirting-- The Approach.

I can remember reflecting on what my approach resembled. I winced thinking about how I froze and how I had such a tough time, even speaking with a woman. Not only that, but when I did get up the nerve to approach women, I found that I didn't have the first hint about how to speak with her or what to discuss. In hindsight, I was going after the entirely wrong woman for me because I hadn't taken note of what I wanted. I felt down and out like I would never get better at this whole dating thing.

At that time, though, I recognized that I needed to be sincere with myself, and I was. I got hard on myself in the sense that I wished to grow, and I decided that this was the time to do it.

Taking Responsibility For Your Life-- Stop TheExcuses!

All set to start getting real? This is where you stop getting in your way. This is where you take responsibility for your life. Own it like a real guy. You will have to stop justifying or making reasons or validating things as being the outcome of outdoor elements. You probably don't think that you're guilty of this, but we've all done it in the past. This simply might be the type of habits that is keeping you from getting what you truly want-- women !!!

If You Give Into The Excuses, Then You Are Only Hurting YourselfHarming

Let's start with a little sincerity and stock here and look at what has caused you to get to where you are. Sure, a lot of us aren't just good at talking to women, though with practice and the right skills, this can be changed. Admittedly, it can be a very intimidating thing, and we struggle to figure out just what we're supposed to say. I have sat where you are right now and felt that seclusion and aggravation, but you don't have to give in to that anymore. Discussion is hard enough, so flirting is like it's a world away.

Believe about what happens from the time you approach a woman to the time she turns you down.

Since you have to break down the whole interaction, this is where it all gets real. Since this is the only way you are going to get much better, don't fear it but face it. Think about what goes on from the minute that you attempt to speak with her. Do you even attempt to approach her, or do you simply put that off? When you are talking to her, are you trying to overcompensate or be someone that you think you should be? Do you become a bumbling idiot? If it's always her fault or just "not the best time," then you know that you have some reasons to deal with it. Yeah, I know no one wants to take the blame off of someone else and put it on themselves; however, it has to be done.

What would you change that you think might make a distinction with women?

Believe about the encounter as a whole and believe about what you may be blamed for the wrong reasons:

If you're sincere, you can typically cut through the clutter to see what kind of excuses you keep going to. These are the things that are holding you back! These are likely contributing factors if you are always blaming the woman or the timing or whatever else. If you simply sit it out because you make sure that she's going to say no, then you are shooting yourself down before you even get an opportunity.

If you are blaming other men for "taking" the hot girl that you saw first, that's another reason. If there are things that you can point to every single time which you make sure are to blame for you not getting the woman, then you need to give up the blame game and rise to your responsibility! Excuses won't take you anywhere, but they will stop you from getting what you desire, so do away with them.

What are you genuinely looking for in a woman? Be truthful here too, and go beyond just "a hot one."

What do you think that a woman like that is interested in?

How can you be a man that women are drawn in to and thinking about?

How can you stand out from the crowd and win women over?

What does flirting mean to you, and how can you get much better at it? How do you think that flirting can help you to win a woman over?

Yeah, I understand it's a lot of questions, and you don't have to answer all of them. The only thing is, though, that if you want to change your approach and your result, you need to analyze what has been happening. Being truthful with yourself is the only way to get to the heart of the woman.

I dealt with it too once you reveal the roadway obstructs and the problems that have been holding you back, then you can get to the beautiful things. There's some excellent stuff too-- think of the thrill of experiencing a successful flirt! Nothing improves your ego and confidence rather than it. You will astonish yourself at how your approach can take shape and how you get the girl—all that by being truthful with yourself and making an effort to look at what has been happening. Yup, the best is yet to come!

Take Note:

- Stop blaming women and other reasons. You are responsible just to yourself.

- Analyzing your unfavorable and favorable techniques to women from the past will assist you in determining what works and what doesn't work in your approach to women.

- Moving forward, when you have discovered the answers, you can develop a plan to overcome the negative and positives of your flirting approach.

The Proper Way and Time To Approach and Make Your Move.

Oh, for the love of God, will you please stop waiting for the right time? Will you stop assuming that this resembles some motion picture where the music is playing in the background as you slowly approach each other, delighting in incredible love at first sight? I'm not saying that it's not possible, I'm just saying that it's not possible. If you continue to waste your life waiting for that perfect moment or that best situation to come, then you are going to be waiting for an extended period and miss many opportunities. Yes, even men can get caught up in the idea of a perfect scenario to meet their dream woman, but you need to come down to earth here, my friend!

You can give yourself a million excuses for why you don't wish to approach her today. It may be that you aren't feeling on top of your game. You might tell yourself that you are sick of rejection. Maybe you just feel like "hanging with your boys," or it may be that you are okay single. Does any of this sound familiar? Yup, we've all existed since we all desire the stars and the moon to be lined up so that we can approach this woman without being shut down. Sounds excellent in theory? In practice and truth, though, this is just not how it usually works.

Sad but true! Women don't always wait on that one right sign, so why are you doing that to yourself?

I get it, working up the nerve to approach a woman isn't always easy. I comprehend it takes courage, and getting rid of that fear of rejection. However, I do know something, though; opportunities present themselves, and you best be on the lookout for them. If you are so deliberate or worry a lot about rejection, then you are losing out. You need to take dangers sometimes to get them to pay off. You need to be willing to put yourself out there. Just what are you so afraid of in the first place?

You'll never know up until you attempt!

It will pass you by if you don't live in the moment at some point in your life. I know how easy it is to just mix into the wall. I understand what it feels like to offer yourself a million reasons or excuses why you shouldn't talk to her. I know that feeling of merely waiting for the "right time" or telling yourself that it doesn'thave to be today. Stop the madness and start focusing on the essential things that matter.

Start searching for methods to seize the moment, get yourself out there, man up and get some courage, and talk with the woman. You'll never know till you attempt, and I promise you that it will be more comfortable with the practice and be worth it!

Here are a few things to assist you figure out how to get that courage and stop getting in your way, perhaps enjoying and getting dates. Yup, you can do this, and the only one stopping you is yourself. The fact hurts, doesn't it, my friend?

Suck it up, buttercup, and go out there and stop fretting about the rejection that you may or might not experience.

Taking Action!

-Know that the right time doesn't exist: Take an action back and let this one sink in. Yes, you're a smart man, and you want good things to occur, but they don't always come in and grab you by the hand. Lean in, more detailed, come on a little bit better, okay, listen to me very thoroughly, and hear what I'm saying perfection does not exist. Mind-blowing, right? Perfect women, perfect relationships, perfect moments-- none of it, excellent must be taken out of your dictionary.

You have to be happy and find your right match, but she's not going to come in the type of pure excellence. So why would you assume that right occurs any longer than perfect relationships? If you sit there and keep waiting on that best moment, you're going to age alone.

Instead, learn that there is no such thing and that you are just making reasons and excuses for yourself. None of which will lead you to anything good. Forget about that right time you have conjured in your mind and just go for it; you've got this!

-Make your right timing and live in the moment: Okay, let's take this one more action, and let this sink in and savor it. You create your own best timing. You get to live in the moment and experience things. You get the pleasure of making your own decisions and letting them work for you. Living means that you delight in how it feels to experience pleasure and even pain. Profound ideas, huh? If you don't experience great hurt, you will not understand what it feels like. If you go through life being merely on the line of blah, you will never get to feel the enjoyment and excitement of flirting and approaching a woman. Yes, the truth is it won't always work out, but then it wouldn't be interesting if you understood it ever would!

The important thing is that you will never understand till you try and though you presume it will be uncomfortable, it might be the start of something great. So make your own "best" time judiciously. Live in this minute and brush aside all the thoughts working against you, then you can talk to any girl you desire.

It's not a match, but you just never know till you try if it's not a game. Go all out, make this your most extraordinary chance, and tell yourself "what the hell" and go speak with her. Just making that decision puts you in control, helps you to be useful in your own life, and for that reason, suggests that good ideas are actual to come your way!

-Go in looking unrehearsed but with a plan of what to say: Okay, this is all about creating actionable steps? I will assist you with "how" and what to focus on, as well as what to say. You can be a very intriguing and intriguing conversationalist. Think about and maybe make a list of questions or topics that you can use so you can walk up to a woman and speak with her.

It may be that you just look at yourself in the mirror and say, "hey tiger, it's high time!". Act and give yourself a pep talk. Try just to act natural, don't worry so much about what you have practiced saying as happen word for word. Bud, it won't happen that way. It's all about having a basic plan of things to discuss with her. It should be as essential as naturally approaching her and just having a few minutes' conversations. You will not have the ability to enter and chat her up right off the bat. You will need practice. So simply attempt some table talk with different women without any result intended. When you have practiced this and feel a bit comfier, you can bring in the more flirty elements.

You don't need a master plan with steps to it, however rather only an idea of what you want to say which you want to do this. Yup, it takes courage, but you've got this, and if you decide that you will do it, then you will hold yourself liable—plan on merely saying hi and asking a bit about her. Don't make it a script, instead just a few general ideas on how to make eye contact and talk with the girl once and for all.

Number one thing on your list needs not to bore her! How are you going to avoid that? That's right-- talk about things she wants to speak about. The essential stuff most men think women wish to hear is not the right topics. Put it by doing this;

Theoretical concern: If a girl came near you, having just read a current list of 'male; discussion topics like a computer game, stock trading, weapons, motorcycles, cars and trucks, sports, virtual truth HD goggles, etc. and begins droning about them, more than most likely you will find a few of it fascinating, but many of it will send you off to the land of nod. It's the very same if you try talking about a basic list of stereotypical 'woman' discussion topics. To find out what she likes talking about, just attempt a fundamental question like, "Hey, what sort of things do you like doing most in your extra time? You are a winner if she seems engaged and starts talking about what she wants.

I'm guessing you are asking now, how do I tell whether what I'm speaking about with the girl is right? Well, let me give you an example of interest and not interested.

Not interested in topic:

Guy: Do you ever make your food?

Ann: No, it looks like a beautiful idea, but I don't have the time.

Guy: Ah, right, yeah, it's tough to find time on your own nowadays. When you are free, what do you choose to do with those precious hours?

Ann is saying here that making her food doesn't intrigue her. So think what Guy, that excellent story you were going to inform her about all your homegrown veg in your kitchen is going to bore her to death. Can you see here how Guy managed to save himself? He altered tact and asked her what she does in her extra time.

Interested in topic:

Guy: Have you been anywhere fascinating overseas just recently?

Ann: Oh my gosh, I just got back from the most fantastic trip to Greece. The Castle was breathtaking.

Ann is incredibly enthusiastic about discussing her journey to Greece. Undoubtedly.

The person is on a winning discussion topic here.

The leading pointer here is to frame any questions that you have, so she needs to address in a manner that doesn't make her seem uncool. And this is not to be carried out in a nasty way, merely a subtle and smart way. Take note of the example of Guy's very first subject that didn't interest her; he framed the second question in a manner that made it difficult for her not to give a more in-depth answer. The method he mounted the matter would have made her wish to address something more refreshing and fascinating. If she answered with something vague like, " nothing much actually," she would seem quite lame and boring. Nobody wishes to be viewed as uncool and uninteresting. And to be honest, if a girl is speaking in this manner, then she is tired of talking to you, or she is dull and not the type of woman you want to put effort into trying to get a date from.

Use unclear, dull responses to your questions is a hint to move on, friend!

-Stop letting your worries get in the way and think about the possible results: I desire you to do something about it in a slightly different method here. I want you to take a seat for a minute and analyze what your real fears are. Yeah, I understand, this is asking you to think and dig deep and deal with things you don't always want to deal with. I promise you that it will bring you some clarity. Stay with me now, and let's face this down together. What are your most significant worries here? What is holding you back?

- Are you scared that she will laugh in your face or turn away from you?

- Are you scared that she will decline you before you even get to speak with her?

- Are you afraid that your ego will get bruised with this trial?

- Do you stay away because you just don't know what to say?

- Are you daunted by her and therefore look like a fool?

- Do you simply worry that you will never get the girl, and so you keep making excuses?

Dealing with down the truth isn't always easy, but it's completely worth it. I'm sure that a minimum of one of these reasons or factors is what's holding you back. Do you understand what each of these worries boils down to when you think about it? Embarrassment. I'm betting it with you that even if among the above does not apply when you discover what you're scared of, it will still boil down to fear of shame. If you allow yourself to see what lies in your way truly, then you can shatter that excuse and progress with a purpose to something spectacular. Because you're about to learn how to produce your own, forget about that right time, and after that, you begin to see that being a great conversationalist and using the correct quantity of flirting is well within your reach. Next, we will look at how to handle the fear of shame.

" Don't wait for the perfect moment, take a moment, and make it perfect."

Note well:

- You can prepare, chart, get scientific or even rely on astrology, but the right time to approach a woman does not exist.

- To discover the right one and also increase your opportunity of getting a date, you need to produce and seize as many chances as possible to flirt and converse with women.

- Increase your possibilities of success by knowing there is no best moment; you create your opportunities, make a basic plan of what to do, and conquer related worries.

Easy Ways To Get Over Your Fear About TheApproach

It's okay to be terrified. Being afraid means, you're about to do something actually, courageous.

Okay, yeah, we're men, we're macho, we're huge difficult men, and we're not scared? Sound like a familiar way society sees our sex? You have likely encouraged yourself that you're not afraid of anything, too, if you are sitting there reading this. You probably have stated to yourself, Not me! No other way, I'm not a sissy. I'm a man, and how could I perhaps get scared by the idea of speaking to a woman? Yeah, I understand, so not you at all. Except that it's a large part of the reason you read this book. You may not always think you are terrified of talking to women; however, you are indeed scared of something. Most likely, a worry of emotional discomfort or shame.

Yes, even us guys get frightened, especially when it concerns rejection. And that's ok. We are genuine; we have feelings too! What we need about all else, though, is to seem like we are respected. I've said it before, and I've said it once again, men require regard. Women long for love and love. Men, we crave and need respect. We want and need to feel respected by our peers and the woman that we're interested in. Try as you may, you can't overlook the truth that regards matters much to you. You have to face the reality you are not always going to feel respected in a dangerous situation like flirting. Because she might not be interested, it may not still work out how you think it needs to, and you might end up feeling disrespected by the woman you are talking to.

In a book by Emerson Eggerichs, the best-selling author of Love and Respect, a sample of men were asked: if required to choose between being left alone and unloved worldwide or to be seen as disrespected and insufficient, which would they prefer? 74% of Emerson's male sample answered they would prefer to be left alone and unloved, whereas the reverse is true of the sample taken from women. While this is a little generalization, and to love a woman, you also require to respect her, it highlights how essential feeling respected is to us.

Feeling respected in a relationship is crucial, but it begins with the time that we fulfill a woman. So if that potential regard is compromised or we think that we will not potentially get it, then we are hesitant about carrying out the regard damaging activity. This is specifically true of the approach and could have been among the underlying reasons that you have been reluctant to do it in the past. For that reason, it's more natural to avoid possible confrontation or hurt feelings by avoiding the approach. You know I'm right. Nevertheless, if you equip yourself with this knowledge and can get ready for the risk, it will be less of a blow if you are declined. And yes, regardless of all exceptional laid plans, it will happen occasionally.

If you're prepared to put in the necessary work, you can get rid of barriers and fears!

Don't let your need for respect and the potential hurt to your ego hold you back! Now let's learn those other possible fears about the approach and get some actionable concepts to conquer them. If you have asked yourself the concerns from earlier in this book, you've currently finished part one of this. However, now it's up to you to take it a step further. Now it's up to you to determine how to get rid of that fear.

Here are some of the likely fears holding you back and the action or steps you can attempt to overcome them.

- You worry that she's going to call you out or reject you: Everyone, men or women, frets about rejection. No one likes it. Simply stop for a minute and ask yourself, so what if she declines you? What's actually the worst that could happen if she chuckles in your face (though I highly question she will)? What will happen in the broad picture of your life if she withstands you or turns you away?

It's not going to be a great feeling. Will your ego be briefly bruised? Yes, it will.

Are you going to go to A&E-- NO!

Are you going to be psychologically scarred for life and need a therapist for life-- NO! It's unreasonable to think that she will push you away or laugh you in your face, so learn that. Know that it's much worse in your mind and brush aside those worries in the meantime.

The truth is that you will not die or be severely impaired in the process. So now think about it again-- What is the worst that can take place? You must be able to address something along the lines of this if you have your positive mindset engaged. At worst, I will feel ashamed for about a half-hour at most. If I'm on my own, nobody needs to know. At best, I come with an amusing story to inform my blossoms and have something word over. I can be honest and real with them and potentially even get some tips from one another. They might then feel comfy enough to share and laugh at their chat up fails with me because of my courage.

It's okay to take a look at how previous errors have shaped you and got you to where you are at today, as long as you are taking a look at them to improve yourself. That's positive. You gain from the mistakes and the unfavorable patterns and concerns; however, they must be in the past. I don't care if you have approached 19 women with a negative outcome because you know what? It only might be that out of the 20th woman that you contacted. She might be the one you were meant to meet. You crashed and burned and got hurt in the past-- so what? You felt like crap and got down on yourself, and now it's over. You're Mr. Positivity!

Summon up that courage that you know is deep down in you. Acknowledge that the only way to conquer you fear to put your plan into action, resolve the past hurt, and leave it there. Move on with purpose. If you enable yourself to experience them, I guarantee you that remarkable things await you.

Getting harmed in relationships becomes part of life. You can't experience love without hurt. Know that it won't take place every single time you talk to a woman or get into a relationship. Brush yourself off and go out there again, my friend. I promise good things will come your way if you attempt to talk to women. You can't die from hurt or shame even if you do crash and burn again. Attempt it and see what works for you.

CHAPTER EIGHT

The Body Language You Must Know if you want to Succeed with Flirting

If You Want TO succeed, the Body Language You Must Know

Read her body movement and search for cues, both favorable and unfavorable: Okay, directly, you will not figure this one out right now. Attempting to read women isn't always simple, and you may look like you need a foreign translator. Which, naturally, you kind of do because it can seem like women are in some cases from a different planet. However, I will help you figure this one out.

Did you know that regardless of it always appearing like it is us men that need to approach to start flirting with women, that 90% of the time it is her? If she is pleased with you approaching her, she will be using motions to propose. This is frequently through face, body, and eye signals sent to the targeted guy. You will more than likely have a hugely successful approach if you are observant enough to pick up on these signals. Now, don't go getting too thrilled by this because most men are not extremely great at detecting female body language. We have so much testosterone floating around our bodies that it can trigger us to often mistaken a friendly smile from sexual interest. What a problem!

If you find out to keep an eye for the hints, a lot of body language is subconscious, and she will be giving tricks from left to right and center. Body language is such a colossal place that an entire book might be committed to it. My suggestion is if you want to know more comprehensive details, to complete your further research.

-Eye Contact: A woman who might be interested in, you will usually look your way, capture your eye for a few seconds, and avert again. Check first your zipper isn't down, and you don't have spaghetti sauce splattered down your shirt as the thing she is looking at. She will repeat this glance up to three times if you are great. Inconsistently looking at you and once again, she has actually proposed her interest in your approach.

-Smiling: All you may get is a fast half-smile. Don't rely on merely a quick smile to show approach. Ensure her other signals show the same.

-Posture: If she wants you to approach, her stance will be set to flaunt. By this, I mean she will be correcting the alignment of clothes, touching or snapping her hair, and perhaps gently licking her lips. If she is sitting down, more than likely, she will be sitting straight-backed with legs crossed, displaying whatever she feels are her best assets. Similarly, if she is standing, she might highlight her curves by tilting her hips a little forward. Remember, with a lot of women, this is subconscious and not what they believe is outright and blatant flirting. Don't go up to her if she is displaying this type of body language, believing she is simple and can be treated. You don't want her to have her impression of you as a sleaze, because you read body movement the wrong way!

-Talking with her: If you are making a great impression after approaching her, she might try to find an opportunity to touch you mistakenly. She may repeat the touch to see how comfy you were with it. Here are some favorable facial gestures to watch out for when speaking to her to boost your self-confidence that your first impression and approach are working out.

o Raised eyebrows: When integrated with a nod or a smile, it usually indicates she is interested and concurring with what you are saying or doing.

o Active eyelids: It's one of the earliest stereotypical female flirts; however, if she is batting her eyelashes at you, she is flirting back.

o Dilated students: this only works in a bright setting. Both boy and girl's pupils dilate (get more extensive and darker) if they are speaking with somebody they are interested in.

o Flared nostrils: This is an involuntary response that happens in females if they are aroused or delighted.

o Lips: Chewing or licking her lips draws your attention towards them, which is a sexual or arousing part of her body.

The things to be cautious of as hints she is not interested in or has changed her mind about you are noted below.

-Crossed arms: If she has passed her arms, chances are she has withdrawn or bored. She is putting a barrier between you both, and you may need to give up trying to flirt and speak.

-Touching her hair in fast jerky movements: Touching hair in slow mild twisting or twirling is a fantastic sign. However, if it's being done in quick, jerky motions, then this means she is uneasy, ashamed, or bored.

-Looking away: When she is interested in you, she will reveal this by looking directly into your eyes. You've lost her if she is looking at everything, but you then its time to give up.

Women can tell you a lot about their interest in you without ever saying a word. Be on the lookout for cues and discover how to produce your own to make this work to your benefit. Not just do you want to learn how to read her, but you also want to work to make your terrific impression. This originates from learning to read body language and likewise build yourself to win her over and show that you are in tune with these things. Remember that this is just a general guide, and not all women have the same body movement. Likewise, sexual gestures like licking lips are carried out unconsciously; allure is the brain's natural reaction if you are interested in somebody of the opposite sex. It does not instantly mean she wishes to make love with you.

Reading her body movement is an excellent tool for you, but remember, she might be doing the very same, so it is essential for you likewise to give the best cues to start flirting and develop a fantastic impression.

Here's a couple of quick tips.

Smile: What have you got to lose in a fast smile? Even if she turns not to be interested, you will have most likely brightened her day. Smiling always makes you feel more favorable and positive.

Upper body: We keep our chest up, and shoulders pointed towards the most crucial thing in the place. So puff it up and keep it in her direction.

Stance: To make yourself look effective, which is sexy to a lot of women, stand with your feet set broad apart and in her direction. You can likewise put your hands on your hips to create a moving image. Practice this in the mirror because you don't want it to be looking dorky.

Touch: She would like to know you are interested too. So if things are going well and you have started discussing, make a thing of flirting by lightly touching her lower back, arm, or waist.

She is probably comfortable with this if she leans in. If not, cease from moving her again till she shows further interest. Girls don't like wandering, creepy hands, so do this with care.

Think about how you desire people to perceive you and the positives that these adds and after that promote it. By this understanding, I mean, do you want to stumble on as the amusing guy; the impeccably dressed guy; the mannered gentleman guy; the outdoorsy guy; the sensitive guy; the quite listening person; the loud outbound person; and so on. Remember, you still need to be yourself, so don't attempt to be the guy you aren't. Work on pressing the angle of your personality that is your selling indicate women in your impression. Put in the work so that someone can't help but go with a good idea of you.

For example, you may now know that you have been trying to put across the funny outbound man in very first impressions, which's not you and what you are comfortable with presenting to women. They will pick this fakeness and get the idea of you as a try-hard. Possibly, you have now listened to the info in previous chapters and taken stock and understand that you are a quiet listener, who is much better at asking interesting questions from the woman they have met. You can now work towards making this the primary thing you will present as favorable in your first impression to women if this is you.

All these features being simple, vulnerable, and sincere, and then putting in the effort to improve it. While you may not like where you are right now, you must be more than ready to give it up.

Be sincere in your assessment and be ready to fix the important things that aren't working for you: If you do think of it, you probably know what isn't working for you. It may be quite apparent, and you never wanted to repair it. You might have felt too overwhelmed to attempt to change up what you knew wasn't favorable for you. Whatever the case might be, sincerity will serve you well here.

I knew that back then, I was not the finest conversationalist, but I faced that down and worked on it. I even became a naturally funnier guy by becoming more at ease in my conversations with women. You can continue to go through life with blinders on, but how is that exercising for you? Be honest in what's not working for you and then put in the work. Enhance the essential things that are creating a tainted or less than a beneficial perception of you. If you can alter that, then you can do anything - and your dating life and first impressions will be favorable from here!

Take note

- First impressions are delicate to get right and need hard work.

- Analyze the type of feeling you are presently making by analyzing past encounters.

To improve or change the type of the first impression you are producing try: getting into their shoes; asking questions to create conversation; reading body movement; figuring out the kind of the first impression you wish to give; being truthful in what need repaired and produce a plan to do it.

Attractive Body Language

As you're reading a book on flirting and talking with women, you most likely wish to have better the ability to draw in women.

Perhaps women seem to dislike you as soon as you open your mouth, maybe you have no clue how to flirt, or maybe you're susceptible to awkwardness.

Whatever the reason, none of that matters if you don't have your nonverbals down pat. You can be the most excellent conversationalist in the world, the world's most practiced flirt, but if you have unsightly body language, you'll be known as scary.

Research studies show that body language has a direct effect on your state of mind, meaning that you can "fool" yourself into feeling incredibly positive, making approaching attractive women a little simpler for you.

Anyhow, let's have a look at how to have women thinking you're a sexy mofo before you open your mouth, as well as how to use nonverbal interaction to make you're flirting more seductive.

BODY MOVEMENT BASICS

" Fie, fie upon her!

There's language in her eye, her cheek, her lip, Nay, her foot speaks; her wanton spirits watch out At every joint and motive of her body."

-- William Shakespeare

Imagine an appealing woman. Picture her sitting with her legs spread large apart ("manspreading," if you will). Envision her also having her hands gripped behind her head, elbows pointing outward. She likewise speaks in a rough, deep, manly voice.

Not so appealing any longer? Why is that?

Men are drawn into feminine women. The woman described above is showing extremely masculine body movement, which we are hardwired to discover unsettling at the best and highly unattractive at worst. Instead, men would find gentle body movement to be more attractive.

Womanly women are drawn into masculine men. They intuitively discover masculine body movement feminine and appealing body movement unsightly.

When you sit with a leg crossed over the knee (like a woman), speak in a high- pitched voice, quickly dart your eyes downward instead of holding eye contact, walk-in fast little actions, and so on, women find that unappealing. Men with feminine body movements are to women what a big, hairy, muscled, deep-voiced lady would be to us men. That is, sexually repulsive.

What does masculine body language look like?

-Expansive.

-Takes more space.

-Terrific posture.

-Slow and purposeful motion (instead of quick, jerky, and unchecked).

-Deep voice (which is done by fully breathing/speaking and unwinding from your tummy, not chest).

-Doesn't smile excessively.

-Swaggers about like a badass. E.t.c.

One of the easiest and essential ways to start embodying the masculine body language is to search for some clips of James

Bond and Marlon Brando and use these men as your body movement function models.

Maybe the best method to establish hot, masculine body language is to get a "body language good example" and replicate them. I 'd recommend either James Bond or Marlon Brando (or both!) as great ones to start with.

When flirting, you wish to lean back and demonstrate that you're relaxed and at ease.

No fidgeting. No "pecking"-- continuously leaning in (and back out again) to hear what she's saying, making yourself look like a bird pecking at food.

Instead, make sure your movements are calm and regulated.

By showing robust body movement, you stumble on as (and feel more) confident, helping to make you're flirting more reliable.

Lesson: Have an open, extensive body movement. The most convenient way to do this is to emulate James Bond's body movement. Gentle body movement will, at best, make you extremely unattractive to women (and, at worst, make you sexually repulsive)-- so make sure that your body movement is always manly. You want your body language to put on that of James Bond, not some flamboyant homosexual.

CHAPTER NINE

How To make the Conversation more Friendly

How To Not Make Her Fall Asleep

Most guys (perhaps you included) ask questions like the following:

"What's your job?" "Where are you from?" "What school did you attend?"

Aside from being so dull, they're more potent than sleeping medication; there's one other issue with these questions: They require no more than one word to answer. "Accountant." "Boston." "Hogwarts."

Above that, with enough drinks, she could mistake herself for being in a job interview. So what's the way out?

There are some remedies, so let's start with the easiest

How To Obtain The Most Bang For Your Question

When you ask questions, dive a little deeper. Ask questions that require not a one-word response (or, worse yet, a mere "yes" or "no"), but a more extended, more profound answer. Aim for a paragraph, not one word.

Here's an example:

Guy: Do you like your job?

Girl: Yeah, it's cool.

At least, you get one word ("yes"); at most, you get three.

Not looking good.

Here's an example of how you might tweak it: Guy: Why do you like your job?

Girl: Well, I love...(blah blah blah)

See the difference?

Al.so takes note that women are emotional creatures (as opposed to men who tend to be more logical). Consequently, you can never go wrong, delving into the emotions behind things.

Here's an example of a lost opportunity to establish an emotional connection with the woman:

Girl: I'm a doctor.

Guy: Oh, wow. Long hours?

Here's an example of a guy who seizes the opportunity and establishes an emotional connection:

Girl: I'm a doctor.

Guy: Wow. What's it feel like to save somebody's life?

Yes, the latter example is a little clunky, but you get the idea.

Which question do you think is going to elicit a more emotionally-charged response (to which the guy might be able to relate to an experience in which he felt similarly), create greater emotional intimacy, and get her talking to the guy with powerful, positive emotions? I think the answer's pretty obvious.

Lesson: Ask open-ended questions and, preferably, delve into her emotions and motivations.

Moving on, let's take a look at whether or not you should even be asking questions in the first.

Statement And Question

1. Fuel the conversation- If you think wrongly, she'll always want to know why you guessed what you did. This gives you more to speak about and fuels the discussion.

2. She'll love finding out about herself- There's just one thing women love more than speaking about themselves, which's hearing others talk about her. Whether you guess wrong or right, she'll love hearing about what it has to do with her that made you do what you did.

3. She'll think you're a genius if you guess right- Well, not literally, but she'll be almightily impressed by your perceptiveness.

4. You appear very positive. When you speak in statements, women naturally perceive you to be more dominant, confident, and bold-- all desirable qualities. You look like more of an alpha male.

5. Develops immediate familiarity- When you've just met somebody, you ask each other many concerns. You speak to each other firstly in a statement when you've been good friends (or family) with somebody for years. Thus, by talking to her in speeches, you fool her subconscious into feeling that you two have known each other for long and are more familiar than you are.

6. Gets rid of interview mode- Firstly, you're not asking questions (i.e., "talking to" her) in the first place. Secondly, when you guess aspects of her, that adds more fuel to the fire, giving you non- interview-y things to speak about.

So when it comes to statement versus question, there's no contest.

To give you a clearer image, here are some more examples:

Question: What do you do?

Statement: You look like an artsy type, I wager you're a [some sort of imaginative job]

Question: Want to grab something to eat?

Declaration: You need to be starving; let's get something to eat.

Question: Want to opt for a walk?

Declaration: Let's go for a walk.

Feel the difference? The statements are more active and dominant. On the other hand, the questions sound practically clingy by comparison, as if you're seeking authorization or are unsure of yourself.

Lesson: Turn questions into declarations. You sound significantly more confident, dominant, and competent. Statements can likewise intensify to the discussion in regards to the excitement and having more things to discuss.

From Dull Questions To Flirty Statements

You don't need to stop there, though. So far, we've gone from dull questions to declarations, but if we add a little bit more spice, we can go from blunt questions to speeches, to flirty statements.

Here's an example of concern, statement, and flirty declaration:

Question: What do you do?

Declaration: You look like an artsy type, I wager you're [some sort of imaginative task]

Flirty Statement: Let me guess. you must be a [drug dealer/exotic dancer/astronaut/etc.]".

Now, you don't wish to continually make out-there guesses like "dancer" or "drug dealer," or it'll be using, and you'll come off like a clown. But you can inject a little extra "spice" into your declarations from time to time to give excitement and generate an amusing back and front.

Lesson: You can always weave a completely ridiculous presumption into your declaration to create some enjoyment. You might likewise suggest something sexual to amp up the flirting and produce some sexual stress.

CHAPTER TEN

Playing the Flirting Game

No matter how much wealth you have and who you are, you must follow some tips and rules to flirt with a stunning girl and to make her your own. Yes, occasionally, you might discover a man who has got a lovely woman. You are to think that it happens seldom, or he is nonetheless a lucky man. On the other hand, you would know some men who try their best to get a stunning woman but end up failing. You need to follow an excellent method for attempting to flirt with girls. This is the essential chapter of this book, and it shows you the way to a great date.

Try to Know What Her likings Are

When you are in front of each other, you can not begin flirting with her unless both of you find comfort. Ask her what her favorite subject is, what kind of music interests her, who is her favorite star, and so on. This type of discussion will make your girl feel easy. Unless she opens up to you, you can not begin flirting with her. Try to agree with her preferences and confess that you also have a taste of her tastes. Program some reasoning behind your choices that might impress her. At last, admire her likings.

Keep it secret

You need to ensure that the woman you are flirting with never becomes aware of what is going on. It is better that she does not understand your plan and mission. If she becomes conscious of your intention, you may need to give up the hope of dating and try to find another stunning girl. That is never good news for you. Try to keep it a secret. Another reason for keeping your plan a secret is that you are going to impress her at any expense, and for this, you need to go through a process. If the woman you desired knows your intention for flirting with her, she will take every of your act in before her as a part of your plan. Then impressing her will become next to impossible. So, you should keep it a secret to flirt with her.

Make Her Smile

Try to be an amusing person but not that amusing to the point of being a clown. Women always choose those men who have a shared sense of humor. The more she smiles, the more she opens to you. For this reason, making your wanted girl smile is essential. There is another benefit of making her smile. When the girl is alone, she may remember you and smile once again. Thus, you may enter her heart. To flirt with a girl, you should get into her heart. You can make some jokes also to make her smile.

Tell Her She is Beautiful

Women are always conscious of their appearance, body, and costumes. Matching them is a good and straightforward way to flirt with them. Whenever you see your preferred girl using a stunning dress, never waste time to tell her that she is looking gorgeous in the dress. Tell her that this dress suits her a lot. It will have a great impact on her. If she uses that dress in another t, your complimentary remark will be remembered, and you will be in her idea. By doing this, you can move another step towards her. Keep getting closer to her and wait for the day you are valuing.

To flirt with your wanted girl, you should always watch her to catch any sort of changes in her look or appearance. For instance, the girl you like may have a new hairstyle. As you see her, you should talk about it. You can also add something like, "You are looking more stunning in this new hairstyle." It will send her a message indicating that you continuously observe her very carefully, and you are quite interested in her. Women like to be followed by men. She will understand that you are not one of those who only know how to say, "You are gorgeous" to impress girls.

Take Her Out

You can take her to someplace for lunch or dinner. Since there will be no nuisance between you and her, it can offer you more time and space. The girl will be pleased. She will also come to understand that you left the friendship zone. You can invite her to enjoy a movie picture with you in the theatre. At the cinema, you both will find a different environment. Make sure that the movie is romantic. If she comes with you to watch a romantic comedy, romantic scenes will move her a lot. She may consider you as her hero and find herself the heroine of that movie.

Appreciate Her Choice

If your preferred woman purchases something new, you must appreciate it. To flirt with her, you can not just stop here. You may tell her that her choice is exceptional and authentic. Tell her that her decision is a proof of her being an exception from other women. Every woman enjoys to present herself as different from other girls. Tell her to help you in choosing things if you want to buy something for yourself. As women like shopping, she may concur with your proposition. You need to buy what she accepts for you. If you do so, it may make her believe that you genuinely like her choices, and you value them. When you both are at the market to buy, if she selects something for her and does not purchase it for an unknown reason, you better purchase it secretly and give it to her the next day. It will shock her most, and women like to be surprised in this way. She will think that you genuinely care for her.

Inform her that you are eager to check her out

If your desired girl comes wearing a really attractive dress, you need to observe her from feet to head. Just keep looking at her. You need to tell her that she is looking hot when she is about to leave. It will make her feel attractive. Women just love this feeling. The more you can provide her with this kind of opportunity of feeling hot, the more you pave the way for dating her.

Using Text

A man can quickly use his phone or social media to flirt with ladies. Try to build up a relationship of exchanging texts with your wanted girl. The language of your text must cross the line. In your texts, call her using the sweet words and try to use her nickname. Whenever you find her phone switched off or she is offline, simply send messages like "Anything wrong?", "Are you OK?" "Miss you." When she is going to open her cellular phone or will be online, she will find your texts and may think about you positively. She will text you back, and therefore interaction will take place so well between you and her. It will help you a lot to flirt with her and win her heart.

You can compare "Flirting a Girl" to a game. In the game, you use some tricks and tips to win, here to win in flirting with women you also need the same procedure and techniques.

Get noticed

You can not get the chance to flirt with a girl unless you get noticed. Your personality, look, smartness will come to no use, if you stop working on getting seen by women. So, getting noticed is nonetheless really essential. Just wearing beautiful clothing and having a cool hairstyle will not help you to get observed unless you use your eyes as a medium of communication and make facial expressions very well. This chapter will tell you about how you can make a woman notice you.

Eye Contact

To flirt with a girl, you need to make eye contact with her through her eyes, and it is essential for your purpose. A correct usage of eye contact can provide you with your required steps for this mission. She will notice you among thousands of people if you can manage an accurate eye contact with a girl. Try to keep your eyes directly to her eyes. Do not take a look at something else until she takes a look at you and finds that you are staring at her. The girl will try to find out what you have to say through your eyes. The more she tries, the more you enter into her head. This is a fantastic benefit for anyone. As it will make her consider you all the time and gradually she might get a special feeling for you. In this situation, your opportunities for dating this girl increases at a high rate.

Staring

We can quickly discover whether a woman and a man sitting in front of us are a couple or not. The lovers use to look at each other in various ways. They do not practice glance; instead, they keep looking at each other for an extended period. While flirting with a girl, keep gazing at her. A prolonged staring will have a terrific influence on her.

When a man gets his desired girl with no one around her, he usually feels like kissing her. If he does so, without any progress in flirting with her, she may get upset. Thus his date can get completed in no time. So, in the beginning, he needs to make her notice about what he is asking for. If you are wise enough, you can do that quickly. In the beginning, look at her lips and eyes. She will be able to know what you are saying if she gets interested in you. As she completes her speech, you just appreciate her speech and kiss her. Now she will not get upset anymore.

Facial expression

You can use your facial expression to get noticed. Whenever you are in front of a lady, keep a lovely expression on your face. Whenever she talks with you, keep your face directly at her. Some individuals have a bad practice of keeping their hands on their faces or looking here and there while talking. You better prevent it. You can bite your lips with your teeth, if you want to make you look a bit serious. You likewise can bring a gentle smile on your face. You need to look at her a couple of times if your preferred girl stands right behind you. However, do not make any obscene expression. Just try to tell her through your declaration that you have started liking her.

How to Get Her Begging to You ASAP

It is important to learn the interesting flirting games that have women passing away to see you once again. Due to the fact that you challenge her in a lively manner, these games can help build connections and make her comfortable.

Challenging a woman is the very best way to create a sexual urge. It tickles the playful side of women. Don't forget that no matter how you challenge her, you need to involve some type of touching.

When dealing with a woman who delights in a lively challenge, simply be sure that the games you play are enjoyable, and you use them.

In specific circumstances, you can get her to really compete with you. This is a great way to build sexual tension. But if you are bad with initiating that level of physical contact, you can begin it with another challenge like who can send out a text much faster.

Just keep in mind that the most crucial guideline for flirting is that you increase the attraction and capture her attention with secret and interest.

CONCLUSION

Here is a fast wrap-up of all the main flirting strategies, techniques, and tips talked about in this book.

Flirting is subtle. You need to indicate attraction, rather than straight-out state it playfully. Create secret, be vague, indicate instead of the state, and, most importantly, be lively.

It is very vital to understand the distinction between friendly small talk and sexual flirting. Flirting is not the same as the fun, friendly small talk you have with your male buddies. Flirting is far more sexual-- not straight sexual (as stated above), but indirect. If you banter with her in a friendly way, you'll most likely than not end up in the friend zone. So ensure you playfully weave in sexual undertones.

When women 'shit test' you, such as by making a rude remark, asking an unpleasant question, or poking and prodding for possible insecurities of yours, just amplify and concur whatever she says.

Act like you're the reward. This is a gratifying and playful method of flirting. Simply reframe the conversation-- or any of her actions as if she is the one chasing after (and trying to seduce) you.

Have a strong frame of mind. This is probably among the essential elements of flirting, because your frame of mind comes everything else.

When you find yourself needing a fast refresher on the fundamentals of flirting, you may review all the strategies in this book and get on your way.

Now. all you have to do is put this book down and start! Best of luck!